Reminiscences of Present-Day Saints

Reminiscences of Present-Day Saints

BY
FRANCIS GREENWOOD PEABODY

WITH ILLUSTRATIONS

Essay Index Reprint Series

BOOKS FOR LIBRARIES PRESS
FREEPORT, NEW YORK

First Published 1927
Reprinted 1972

Library of Congress Cataloging in Publication Data

Peabody, Francis Greenwood, 1847-1936.
    Reminiscences of present-day saints.

    (Essay index reprint series)
    Reprint of the 1927 ed.
    CONTENTS: Ephraim Peabody.--Andrew Preston Peabody.
--James Freeman Clarke. [etc.]
    1. Christian biography. I. Title.
BR1700.P4 1972   209'.22   74-37525
ISBN 0-8369-2576-9

PRINTED IN THE UNITED STATES OF AMERICA
BY
NEW WORLD BOOK MANUFACTURING CO., INC.
HALLANDALE, FLORIDA 33009

TO
F. W. P.

PREFACE

THE word 'Saint' has had a curious history of ecclesiastical limitation. It has been a title given, as a rule, either to the immediate disciples of Jesus, some of whom, according to the record, were not distinguished for saintliness and at the crisis of his fate 'forsook him and fled'; or, on the other hand, to the martyrs or miracle-workers who have in later centuries won the reverence of the Church. *Apostoli, martyres, orate pro nobis*, became the prayer of invocation addressed to the saints.

The New Testament usage was more generous. The 'saints' were simply those who had committed themselves to the cause of Christ, not as exceptionally pious persons or as endowed to work miracles, but as testifying by the conduct of their lives to the influence of their Master. They were 'called to be saints,' 'sanctified in Christ Jesus,' 'called unto holiness,' 'faithful in Christ Jesus.' One of them might be tempted to doubt, another to deny; and the most influential of them confessed such wrestlings of the flesh with the spirit that it might seem strange to give him the title of 'Saint Paul.' Yet the confessedly incomplete, but finally dominating, direction of conduct towards the ideals of Christian living was precisely what gave them the right to be called

v

saints. 'Not as though I had already attained, either were already perfect,' writes Saint Paul, '... but this one thing I do, forgetting those things which are behind, and reaching forth unto those things which are before, I press toward the mark for the prize of the high calling of God in Christ Jesus.' More than sixty times the word 'saint' thus occurs in the New Testament, not as the title of a few beatified souls, but as the general appellation of loyal Christians, and this 'unrestricted application of the term,' it is authoritatively stated, 'survived until the time of Irenæus and Tertullian.' [1]

As I look back on a long life of exceptional privilege and opportunity, I find myself deeply impressed by observing the number of acquaintances or friends who deserve to be remembered, in this New Testament sense, as saints. They were not so designated by any ecclesiastical authority; they would have disclaimed any honorific distinction; they were simply consistent Christians, for whom holiness was but another name for wholeness or health, the dedication of the whole of life to the Christian Way. By the fortunate circumstances of my childhood, education, and professional life, I have been environed by these characters, whose piety was steadied by wisdom and whose gifts were dedicated to service. It has become a fashion of late for biographers to reexamine the lives of heroes or saints, and to expose

[1] Herzog, *Encycl.* v, 670; Smith's *Bible Dict. s. v.*

Preface

the foibles and failings which made them less heroic or saintly, and more like commonplace sinners. It would seem to be quite as legitimate — and certainly much more inviting — to turn in the opposite direction, and apply one's self, not to efface the halos which piety has drawn round undeserving figures, but to realize that, even within the circle of one's own experience or memory, there have been lives, some of them conspicuous and some obscure, which teach one what saintliness means. Much has been written also of late about sinners, great and small; and the records of criminality and self-indulgence have offered alluring material for historians to review and for the daily press to exhibit in nauseating detail. Is it not time to call attention to the dimensions and the dramatic interest of goodness, and to review the evidences, in literature or life, which justify faith in integrity and consecration?

Almost any one could compile a list of such uncanonized saints among the influences which have guided or restrained his life, and the names which I have here brought together are but a few of the many which I am tempted to recall. It has been a problem, not of discovering, but of selecting, subjects of reminiscence. Some of those whom I describe were teachers; some were preachers; some were men of affairs; one was a soldier; one a statesman; one a Wall Street merchant; one a country school teacher; two were women; but from them all,

Preface

as from stars of greater or less magnitude, there
radiated illumination and beauty; and it has seemed
to me possible that others might be reassured, as I
have been, by observing, through the clouds of materialism and commercialism that drift across one's
sky, how secure and undimmed the stars remain.
Laurence Oliphant once said that what England
most needed in his time was 'a spiritually-minded
man of the world.' That is the type of character
which I here recall. It confirms one's faith in what
the Christian Church has called the 'Communion of
Saints'; not of saints detached from the world, but
of men and women of the world who could interpret
its transient incidents with the serenity and insight
of spiritual minds.

These figures range themselves in my memory
along my own path of life, as though at each of its
turnings or crossings one of them stood, to direct or
deter or lead the way; and as I approach a study of
their characters, I am led to review the occasions
when I fell in with such trustworthy guides. The
result is not an autobiography, but a series of dis-
connected sketches. Personal experiences are narrated when they make points of contact with lives
more deserving of record; circumstances of acquaintance or friendship serve as frames in which to set
Reminiscences of Present-Day Saints.

CONTENTS

ILLUSTRATIONS

Reminiscences of Present=Day Saints

CHAPTER I

EPHRAIM PEABODY

I MUST have been a very backward little boy, for I was nearly seven years old when my father died, and I can remember hardly anything of his appearance or his teaching. He was, it is true, slowly dying through the last two years of his short life, and his children were lodged with friends while he vainly sought by change of climate to arrest the progress of insidious disease. Yet it would seem that one who so profoundly impressed other lives, both old and young, must have given some farewell counsel which even the youngest of his children could never forget, and that something more than a gaunt figure in the high pulpit of King's Chapel, and a hushed and darkened home of sorrow, should remain as personal reminiscences.

The only vivid recollection which survives of worship during my childhood in the beautiful old church is of so frivolous a nature that it should perhaps be resolutely forgotten; yet it persists in recurring whenever, after seventy years, I glance upward at the noble Corinthian columns and their ornate capitals. Round the ceiling of the chancel are ranged a series of projecting and decorated brackets, known, I believe, in the language of Greek architecture, as modillions; and the intervening

I

spaces seemed to the discerning eyes of a little boy created to serve as stalls where one might keep a stud of imaginary horses. Perched on a high cricket and propped against my mother's knees, my eyes looked upward with a fixity and rapture of gaze which may have indicated to my family a precocious piety, but which was in fact watching my chariots, as they emerged from their little stalls and raced round the track laid out on the ceiling of the entire church. In so entrancing and exhilarating an occupation no sermon seemed too long, and my only apprehension was that the closing hymn might be announced before I had safely stabled my panting steeds.

There would, therefore, seem to be slight justification for including among these reminiscences of saints the meagre memory of so remote a figure, or of so infantile a preoccupation. Yet, in fact, the influence of my father's character was felt by his children with imperative command long after he died, and the parental guidance which I just failed to receive was revived and perpetuated through the unremitting devotion of his remarkable wife. She was born and bred under conditions very different from those of her husband; a cultivated, gay, and luxury-loving girl; but she subdued her buoyant temperament to his serene and serious spirit, and, being left a widow, in middle life, with a young family, made it her daily rule and practice to direct her home as he would wish. Each morning began with family prayers; each Sunday demanded attendance at two services of worship with an intervening Sunday School, and a gathering at twilight for the repeating of hymns and Bible passages. Each child must offer a fresh chapter for recitation, and there was much scrutiny devoted by the children to the discovery of the shortest Psalm.

The effort thus to remould her lively temperament for this graver task made my mother's discipline more rigorous than my father's gentle spirit might have enforced. All was for his sake; each decision of school or play was as he would have desired; and while his living presence grew dim, the memory of him remained vivid and imperative through this vigorous fulfilment of his slightest wish. Thus my boyhood was in a singular degree directed by an invisible influence and restrained by a transmitted memory. The conduct of life — as, for example, in abstinence from tobacco — was dictated by the wish of my father, reported to me by my mother, that I should not smoke while in college; by the end of which term of prohibition the habit had lost its persuasiveness — a loss which I have to confess deprives me of one comforting solace of old age. I hardly know which parental influence was more imperative — the intimation of a father's wishes or the dictation of a mother's will. It is a pathetic memory of family life that for a score of years

3

Thanksgiving Day was never celebrated in our home because it was the day on which my father died. The crayon portrait by Cheney hung before the family in our living-room and seemed to watch us all with serene and searching eyes, like a living presence of chastening and refining love; and these memories seem to justify me in recalling my father's influence as immediately controlling, even though indirectly felt and vicariously enforced.

Nor can I dismiss these memories of childhood without testifying to the singularly good fortune it was for a boy to be born and bred in the home of a consecrated parish minister. It is sometimes suggested that ministers' sons are likely to be repelled by the excessive piety of their environment, and to remember the inhibitions of their childhood rather than its inspirations. Nothing could be more unjust to the great majority of these devout and consistent homes; and least of all where the memory of the father had become a great part of the mother's religion. My mother was left with four maturing children and with very restricted means, yet every opportunity of education was secured for her children, and every instinct of domestic unity and affection was quickened and confirmed. The youngest boy had his full share of sidewalk-shovelling and boot-blacking, on a wage scale which was rather to be regarded as a honorarium than as a compensation; and among the family traditions there long remained the tale that when a bucket of water must be carried upstairs and some one suggested a little 'filthy lucre' might be of assistance, the small boy — none too scrupulous in the use of water for personal hygiene — retorted that he was quite willing to do the work but protested against being called bad names.

Most of my playmates were from luxurious homes; but I cannot recall any sense of contrast or inclination to envy. Healthy boys are, in fact, the most consistent of democrats. They do not really care for distinctions which grown-up people observe. Many of the elaborate entertainments provided by my companions on Beacon Hill were repressed by the presence of maids and butlers; and there was quite as much hilarity among us when we sat at my home on the rug before the fire, and munched nuts and apples. Our only heroes were the boys who could run fastest or play most fearlessly, and indifference to finery was a part of self-respect.

Much more notable than this reminiscence of pure democracy was the stamp set on childhood by a home full of books. My father had indulged himself, during a short journey in Europe, in collecting some illustrated descriptions of places and galleries; and, like most ministers, he had acquired from grateful parishoners a few well-bound volumes. The real education of a little boy thus began, not in the completely mechanical routine of the dame-school, but in the untutored intimacy with good books half understood, and good pictures half appreciated. The hearthrug was my academy, and the 'Musée Français,' 'Women of the Bible,' or 'Roman Antiquities,' my textbooks ; and the pupil in that school of the eye and heart, sprawled before the fire, dragged down his guides from their shelves, and made the grand tour of Europe on his stomach. Thirty years later, when I reached Athens, I was almost startled to have a feeling of being at home and knowing my way, and to recall that I had often inspected the monuments and climbed to the Acropolis with my father's big books as the Baedekers of my imagination. Nothing that school or college can do to wake a young mind — and their effect is often soporific — can compare with these fireside travels through the fairyland of art, or the listening to poetry, even when but half understood, at 'that best academe, a mother's knee'; and when this unforced, and often unconscious, education is through the books which one's own father has gathered with such affection and self-restraint, literature and life unite as masters, and the boy learns not by rote but by heart. Reflections like these tempt one to confuse hearsay with memory and to report as reminiscence what may be in fact tradition.

EPHRAIM PEABODY was born in 1807 at Wilton, New Hampshire, and died at Boston in 1856, at the

Ephraim Peabody

age of forty-nine.[1] His father, another Ephraim, was at once village blacksmith, justice of the peace, selectman, and in 1815 a member of the State Legislature. The work of the smithy was a training in integrity and force. This stalwart craftsman won as his wife the daughter of the village squire, Abiel Abbot, and brought her from the ancestral home on Abbot Hill to a house on the 'Intervale,' still picturesque even in decay, under a majestic elm on the bank of a lovely river, and held together by nails shaped by the builder's own hands. The marriage was a union of two unadulterated English stocks, inheriting the tradition of Puritanism for a century and a half, and trained in the pious simplicity of rural New England.

In 1816, the husband, though but forty years of age, died, and his widow Rhoda, a woman of severe beauty, determined will, and with a lurking sense of humor detected in her deep-set eyes, but retreating as if ashamed, was left to rear her two children, a son and a daughter. Puritan thrift relieved the little family from any sense of poverty, and Puritan habits disguised affection. Rhoda's son once said, in recalling his childhood, that he could not remember his mother ever kissing him ; but, on the other hand, wrote that 'he never knew her to show symptoms of impatience or anger,' and in a letter to her from

[1] The story is told in greater detail in 'A New England Romance.' Houghton Mifflin Company, 1920.

7

college, 'Your children owe more to you a thousand fold than they can ever repay.'

At the age of thirteen Ephraim was sent to Phillips Academy, Exeter, where his mother's cousin, Benjamin Abbot, was head-master; and three years later, in 1823, he entered Bowdoin College, graduating in 1827, at the age of twenty. Here was soon touched the note in his disposition which was to become most characteristic and dominating. He was by temperament, and often by a spiritual compulsion of which he was but half aware, essentially a poet; imaginative, reflective, and observant of nature and life. Even in his childhood, as his boyish diary recorded, he would lie on his back to watch the flight of partridges; and in late manhood, when calling the attention of a friend to a summer cloud, he said: 'How often when I was a boy have I thrown myself on the ground and watched such a cloud as that, expecting to see the faces of angels leaning over its edge.'

James Martineau, in a classic paragraph, has not hesitated to affirm 'the close affinity, perhaps ultimate identity, of religion and poetry'; and it must be admitted that the poets have gained a permanence in religious influence which the theologians can hardly claim. Dante remains an interpreter of the soul's wanderings while the popes and dignitaries of his day are remembered only if mentioned by him. Milton has outlived Laud. Wordsworth teaches the religion of nature to many who are unresponsive to the doctrines of the Church. The religious mood of the Victorian era was more clearly uttered by Tennyson and Browning, and its questionings by Arnold and Clough, than by the academic expositors or critics of their day. John Henry Newman is familiar to millions through his 'Lead, Kindly Light,' to whom his defence of authority makes no appeal.

It was this way of self-expression which opened before the young mystic, Ephraim Peabody. The magazines and societies of Bowdoin College offered him a channel of utterance, and the romantic poets of his time, Gray, Cowper, and Wordsworth, directed its course. He contributed reflective essays and verses to the 'Escritoir,' a college journal of brief and languishing life, on subjects like 'A Night in the Woods'; he delivered a 'Poem in Spenserian Stanzas' at a society of college mates; and as his Commencement part he gave a poem entitled 'The Becalmed Ship' — a title curiously suggestive of the temporary lack of determined course which is not infrequent in young men about to graduate from college.

Among these boyish flights of imagination, which often betray a limited or unassimilated experience, the only lines which have met the test of time are, as might be surmised, the ones which are least concerned with Wordsworthian reflections. His

'Skater's Song' has the agility and momentum of real experience, and it has been lately welcomed, essentially as it was written, as material well adapted for musical setting. Indeed, the verses give a pleasant indication that the ascetic student was not without his share in the athletic joys of a normal youth.

'Away, away, o'er the sheeted ice,
　　Away, away, we go ;
　On our steel-bound feet we move as fleet
　　As deer o'er the Lapland snow.

.　.　.　.　.　.　.　.　.　.　.　.　.　.　.　.　.　.　.

　'But as for me, away, away,
　　Where the merry skaters be,
　Where the fresh wind blows and the smooth ice glows
　　There is the place for me.'

Bowdoin College recognized the young poet, and twenty-five years after his graduation, in 1852, he gave the poem at the semi-centennial of the College. Harvard College also appreciated his gift, and in 1835 he was appointed poet of the Phi Beta Kappa Society. In a word, the sense of kinship between religion and poetry grew more vivid and sustaining as his thought and life grew more mature.

A striking evidence of the unconsciousness with which this gift for poetry may be possessed was later given when, at the close of Ephraim Peabody's life, a collection of his sermons was made, selected in great part by himself, and posthumously published. Both he and his affectionate editors were tempted to regard as most important and typical his contributions to the theological thought of his time, and they set in the foreground of this volume his discourses on 'Miraculous Interposition,' 'Authority,' 'The Resurrection of Christ,' 'Nature with and Without a Revelation of Immortality,' to which, no doubt, he had given his most laborious reflection. Many a teacher or preacher has been thus inclined to estimate as his best work what was hardest for him to do, and to fancy that his arguments would be more convincing than his visions. The fact is, however, that the most permanent teaching is likely to be conveyed by the most unintended self-expression, and that a lyric of the soul may outlive a proof of God. 'If a man were permitted,' said Fletcher of Saltoun, 'to make all the ballads, he need 'not care who should make the laws of a nation.' If a man, it might be said to the same effect, be permitted to report his own experience of the life of God in the souls of men, he may leave to others the defence of theism.

So it was with this poet-preacher. When one turns back to this volume, published seventy years ago, the argumentative discourses which involved such exacting toil are seen to have lost their interest or even their validity, while the lyric themes which were more congenial to the writer still speak the timeless language of the spirit. 'The Voice Behind Thee,' 'Stillness of Mind,' 'Stand in thy Lot,' 'The Lamps are Gone Out,' and, more than all,

'Chambers of Imagery' — are still cherished by readers who recognize in them the kinship of religion with poetry. 'Come,' says the last of these sermons, 'and by that door to which all have the keys enter these halls of imagery within the human soul. Light up the torches and raise them aloft that we may see what is upon the walls.' That was a summons to self-scrutiny which was not of one period of theological thought, but as timeless as the beauty of holiness or the ugliness of sin.

Even a theological sermon is relieved in its argumentation by the lighter touch of the poet. Thus in his defence of 'Miraculous interposition,' he says: 'The mariner drifts day by day on the ocean in the midst of a summer calm; the night sinks down over the tranquil waters. No sound comes from the sea; but at night the winds break forth and the mountainous waves chase each other toward the rocky shore. Suddenly the stroke of a bell is heard — scarce heard at first, but louder and ever louder — tolling, pausing, tolling, ringing — its strange chimes blending with the storm and heard, now low, now loud, amid the fury of the gale. The established order which the mariner had observed was silence. He knew not that wise foresight had hung by the coast of peril this voice, silent when all was peaceful, but which, when the storm beat and the waves rose and danger threatened, should be ready to clang forth its warnings. Would this be a violation of law?

Ephraim Peabody

No, only a variation of the accustomed order, produced by causes not coming forth into action until the appointed moment had arrived.'

With these gifts of a poet and this training of a Puritan, Ephraim Peabody was inevitably led from college toward the vocation of the ministry, and after three arid years of theological curriculum in the Harvard Divinity School he proceeded to what was then the frontier town of Meadville, Pennsylvania; thence to the larger pastoral responsibility of New Bedford, and finally to Boston. Twenty years before his death symptoms of pulmonary disease had appeared, and just before the day of his Phi Beta Kappa poem at Harvard University, in 1827, a hemorrhage foretold his doom. In his time, the attitude, even of intelligent people, toward the approach of tuberculosis was not that of resistance, but that of resignation. Ephraim Peabody, with the frame of a blacksmith and the clean inheritances of a Puritan stock, might in all probability have recovered his strength under the modern treatment of sunshine and invigorating climate; but in his generation, when the signs of susceptibility asserted themselves, the only reasonable use of remaining life was to mitigate and prolong the preparation for death. The sedentary habit of a minister's life contributed to this decline of vitality. Scientific precautions might perhaps have fortified his constitution; but the persistent symptoms had for him the

13

mark of inevitable destiny. He found temporary relief by migrating to Mobile, where, he wrote, 'he threw off disease as a garment in the open woods of Alabama.' But the garment clung to him and the solitude depressed him, and with his brave wife he migrated back to New England and had seven happy years in New Bedford, and ten more at King's Chapel before he completely surrendered, in 1856, to merciless disease.

It is not impossible that this consciousness of an impending fate contributed to stimulate his intellectual activity. Articles in the 'North American Review,' then the most important organ of New England culture, testified to his eager thought. The organization of the Boston Fraternity of Churches was in large part through his efforts, and the records of the Boston Provident Association testify that it 'chiefly owes its origin to him.' Yet it was not through these conscientious undertakings of social amelioration that he gained his influence over the congregation he served; but by the indisputable evidence he gave of a life in habitual communion with the Eternal. It may be that his manifest invalidism intensified this impression of spirituality. The progress of tuberculosis is not infrequently accompanied by an intensity of gaze and a stimulation of faculties, as though the soul looked with less hindrance through the bars of the body. Such was the testimony of many observers concerning the last years of Ephraim Peabody, and this impression is confirmed by the gracious and ascetic features which his portrait presents. 'His eyes,' one friend wrote of him, 'open to you like the great ocean under the gentle and solemn stars'; and another listener described him as 'so gentle and so grave it might be thought one of the old Puritans, leaving his austerity behind and keeping his righteousness, had appeared in our generation.'

A further trait became in these last years conspicuous which might have seemed inconsistent with so unworldly a character. It was a surprising endowment of wisdom concerning affairs of this world, not derived from what is called worldly experience, but from the observation of that experience with detachment and horizon. It was like the survey which an aviator makes as he looks down on the ground plan of a town, and notes, as those walking below cannot, the line of its avenues and open places and the spots of its congestion and crookedness. It was the 'wisdom which is from above,' discerning and direct, of things below. 'In one respect,' a friend wrote of him, 'he was the most remarkable man it has been my fortune to meet; and that was in the union of a childlike simplicity with a singular knowledge of men. His judgments of the characters of those with whom he came in contact were really wonderful. All shams, all pretence, all mere outside coverings seemed to fall at once before his mild eye; and although his opinions were invariably announced with great caution, and he always took the most lenient view possible, it was clear that he understood perfectly the real character of those whom he knew.' Thus it was that men of the professional and business world turned to this unsophisticated, but clarified, mind, and made it their counsellor and confessor. 'It was sometimes difficult,' a colleague said, 'to understand how he acquired such an influence. He was not a man of extraordinary learning, yet it was impossible to be with him and not be influenced by his opinions. . . . The secret of his power was in his honesty, simplicity, and wisdom. He was the most extraordinary judge of character it was ever my fortune to know.'

It is curious to find in one of Ephraim Peabody's sermons a recognition of this faculty of insight which he would have been the last to claim for himself. 'Who has not,' he says, 'again and again seen ordinary minds under a powerful religious influence rising almost to the level of genius? . . . A good conscience sometimes seems almost identical with wisdom. Who has not seen ignorant men, quite incompetent to defend their opinions, possessing an almost fatal certainty of judgment, especially in regard to the moral character both of ends and men? The secret of it was that they were seeking only what was right, and in seeking what was right they have taken the shortest road to what is wise.'

Ephraim Peabody

This lucidity of mind, free from all blur of self-interest, gave to his conversation a singular transparency and insight. 'It was,' a brilliant colleague has said, 'a continuous, unpremeditated overflow of clear, sparkling, gentle waters. It appeared as if his mind, having filled up with its natural variety, quietly let it ripple over the margin of his lips. It was not a talk, but a release of ideas. He let the mirth of others break into his lapsing talk like the occurring of ripples in a serene course. But his mind seemed most naturally engaged in the equable diffusion of its own surplus, and to deposit golden instructions and suggestions by the way, not to leap wide in flashes nor to settle in dark places.'

Such, in brief outline, were some of the characteristics of this unassuming and inconspicuous minister of Christ, who was invalided before he was forty, died when only forty-nine, and was never distinguished for learning or leadership. 'He was,' as his more eloquent friend George Putnam said, 'not always an impressive preacher, not being largely endowed with those gifts of temperament which constitute a born orator. . . His reliance was upon what he was utterly unconscious of — the apostolic gravity, simplicity, sincerity, and weight of his own presence and character. He wist not that his face shone.'

These traits of serene wisdom are fortunately preserved in a second volume, edited by a close friend after Ephraim Peabody's death, and which has had a very different fate from his collection of sermons. The more formal discourses, like most homiletical treatises, have had their day of vitality, and now rest on dusty shelves among the remains of dead books. On the other hand, the little volume known as 'Christian Days and Thoughts,' following in its plan the cycle of the 'Christian Year' which the ritual of King's Chapel observed, has had a continuous vitality, and is still prized in many homes as a manual of devotion. An interesting evidence of its catholicity was provided many years after Ephraim Peabody's death, when a bishop of the Protestant Episcopal Church received a letter from a correspondent who was quite unaware that the author of this little book was not of that communion, urging its republication as an aid to faith. In short, the poetic gift which in his earlier years Ephraim Peabody had expressed without distinguished success in versification, had at last found its open channel of utterance in lyric prose; and the dictum that religion is essentially akin to poetry was verified by analogies and figures in which the struggles and victories of Christian experience were graphically portrayed.

Thus, at the beginning of the New Year, he says: 'Life is a journey. The analogy runs out into particulars. On the journey most of the time is spent in travelling a previously selected road. But at intervals we come to a parting of the ways — ways widely divergent and leading to very different ends ; and we must choose which we will take. At one of these landmarks we stand to-day. We do not make it an occasion ; already in the order of things it has been made so by Providence. . . . Here you stand at the parting of the ways ; some road you are to take ; and as you stand here it is for you to consider how it is that you intend to live. As you review the past, there are many positive evils which you know ought to be left behind. Carry no bad habits, no corrupting associations, no enmities and strifes, into this new year. Leave these behind, and let the dead past bury its dead.'

Again, in urging moral discipline, he says : 'To make a catalogue of duties is not to insure their performance. They are but the foam on the beach which shows how high the tide rises, but does not make it rise.' Or yet again, in describing the way of God with man, he says : 'It does not substitute a foreign virtue, like foreign fruit on dead branches ; it puts life into the trunk, that it may bear fruit of itself. What agencies have concentrated themselves upon the flower in the meadow ! The chemistry of the soil, the rains drifting up from the far-off sea, the sunlight bathing the roots in benignant warmth, the revolution of the seasons — all conspire to un-fold this humble life. So the human soul lives in the midst of Divine help.'

On the other hand, this love of imagery came in his last years to seem a temptation, rather than an endowment, and as likely to obscure, rather than to illuminate, his thought. 'As years advanced,' a friend wrote of him, 'and life grew very serious, he seemed to grow jealous (many would think morbidly jealous) of the imaginative tendencies of his mind, and of the rhetorical embellishments of thought and style in which originally he took delight.' One sign of failing vitality was this distrust of his finest gifts.

In a word, the short life of Ephraim Peabody illustrates in an unusual degree the pervasive and enduring influence of sheer saintliness. If it be true that poetry is more an ally of faith than argument, it is not less true that character is more convincing than creed. The 'Evidences of Christianity' which made Ephraim Peabody's textbook have become superseded or forgotten; but the 'Christian Days and Thoughts,' remains as timely as ever; and many a modest pastor, disheartened because he has no better gift to offer to his people than the consecration of moderate talents, may find himself fortified and reassured by this influence of a self-effacing minister on many hearts and homes.

A week before Ephraim Peabody died, he wrote a farewell message to his congregation: 'I want you to believe that every word I have uttered to you has been spoken with the most intense conviction that the only permanent happiness of this life, the only

Ephraim Peabody

true hope for the life to come, is to be drawn from a religious consecration of one's self to God, and to the performance of the duties which He in His love appoints. I would impress this on you if it were possible with my last words. Now that I stand on the brink of that river (not always dark), I wish that my farewell words may be those which I have expressed in preceding years, when that could be no more than an object of faith which is now becoming a reality.' As the things which were seen proved temporal, the things which were not seen became more clearly recognized as eternal; and what had been an object of faith became a convincing reality. It was the testimony which, through the whole history of the Christian religion, has been given by those who are 'called to be saints.'

CHAPTER II

ANDREW PRESTON PEABODY

I PROCEED from the experiences of childhood to those of youth, and recall the influences which sixty years ago were met in college by a boy who called himself, with playful exaggeration, a student, and which were organized to convert such a boy into a man.

Nothing is easier to propagate than a myth, if it be once securely rooted and repeatedly watered. The class in Harvard College which graduated in 1869 cannot, if its list of members be scrutinized, be fairly regarded as of extraordinary distinction. We had among us one intellectual prodigy, who had lost his right arm in fighting for the Confederacy, and who came straight from a hospital to the hostile environment of the North; but he died in 1877 among strangers, in Algiers, with his promise un- realized through the very versatility of his gifts, and a half-dozen vocations confidently undertaken and lightly discarded. We had also one irresistibly charming classmate, an artist, journalist, adventurer, and companion of princes, who had enlisted at the age of fifteen as a drummer boy in the Civil War; was a captivating companion in college; had won as a painter most of the prizes at Antwerp, and later became distinguished as a venturesome traveller

Affectionately yours,
A. P. Peabody.

and war correspondent. When in later years it was asked where Frank Millet might be found, it was sufficient to name that spot on the earth's surface, in Turkey it might be, or Russia, where at the moment there was the most chance of a revolution or a fight. He was the tent-mate of Skobeleff at Plevna, and was decorated for his services both there and with Gourko at the taking of Sofia. His death at the sinking of the Titanic was like his life, gallant and generous. He calmly watched the women and children depart and waved them a smiling farewell.

It would be difficult to claim many other classmates of great distinction. William Bull, whose college career had been so involved in pranks that he was almost continuously under suspension, became a famous surgeon; and Henry Marion Howe, whose fame in college was derived from an untiring and ingenious proclivity for practical jokes, became the leading metallurgist of this country, from whose name there dangles in the Quinquennial Catalogue a long list of medals and degrees. There remained a sprinkling of professors, one governor of a commonwealth, some lawyers, doctors, and financiers of repute, and the first negro to receive the bachelor's degree at Harvard; but for the most part we were of modest gifts and doings, though, perhaps, not deserving the comment of a clever member of the class of 1868, that the boys of the next year were good but dull. Yet, by a persistent enthusiasm and a lifelong loyalty, the myth has become firmly planted among university traditions that nothing in our generation was of quite so exalted a character as the class of 1869. Other classes cheer us when our surviving members present themselves, and if there be no other sign of appreciation, we cheer for ourselves. The bond of intimacy, instead of slackening with the years, has grown more compelling and affectionate, and as one of our members has said, 'we draw each year closer round the table at our annual gathering, and hold each other's hands.'

In one respect, however, the class of 1869 held a unique position in Harvard history. We stood at the end of an era — the last victims of the penal system which had for two centuries controlled academic life and was ironically described as a liberal education. It is a sufficient indication of the transition to say that President Eliot was inaugurated in the same year in which we received our degrees. Harvard College might have accepted as its motto in 1869 the great words of the Apostle Paul: 'Old things are passed away; behold all things are become new.'

It is true that Josiah Quincy, in his presidency ending in 1845, had introduced what President Eliot later called a 'rudimentary elective system'; but he was succeeded by five estimable scholars, all of whom had been bred in the classics or in theology, and who for twenty-three years directed a reversion to scholastic conservatism which made the curriculum of the College indistinguishable from the standardized system of a preparatory school. Indeed, the College at that time was no larger than many schools are to-day, having less than five hundred students and an endowment hardly exceeding two million dollars. Latin and Greek were the staple food for young minds, with a smattering of ethics, 'American' political economy, and physics, for flavoring. The rules governing a student's life were those of a reformatory. Smoking in the College yard was a crime, as was the offence defined as 'grouping,' a group being any number more than two persons. At 6:45 in the autumn and spring, and at 7:45 in winter, the summons to pray dragged a half-clothed mob through the dark to the chapel, where proctors sat along the sidelines to watch for indecorum or insufficient attire, and monitors stood up, with their backs to the pulpit, to check absentees.

It is a curious fact, and should be credited to these classical and clerical administrators, that there were gathered in their time at Cambridge some of the most distinguished scholars in America. One might meet at any corner a great man of science, Louis Agassiz, Jeffries Wyman, Asa Gray, or Benjamin Pierce; or a light of literature, Longfellow or Lowell; or a master of classical learning, Goodwin or Lane. Yet the still more curious fact must be added that, except for some selected disciple, like Charles Eliot under J. P. Cooke, not one of these academic stars shed any light on the narrow path of the undergraduate. Agassiz, Wyman, and Lowell shone upon us only in a few incidental lectures. Pierce was so remote a planet as to be visible only to a few telescopic minds. Under Asa Gray's kindly instruction, spring flowers were brought to be identified in the classroom; but the class of 1869 learned the names, for the most part, not by analysis, but by nudging the elbows of the boys who lived in Concord. To commend one's self to the learned classicists, Goodwin and Lane, it was more essential to detect an aorist tense or an irregular verb than to appreciate Euripides or Terence.

In a word, we were schoolboys, chiefly concerned with memorizing rules and exceptions, regimented in recitations, and without training of the eye or hand. We studied chemistry without ever touching a test-tube and physics without approaching a laboratory. Indeed, the experiments in the latter science were so archaic that the successor of our teacher, being asked what had become of the apparatus with which Professor Lovering entertained our class, replied that not one of these illustrations of science was, twenty years later, anything but a historical curiosity. The same antique methods prevailed in all our classrooms, where even gifted teachers were primarily devoted to the discovery of deficiencies rather than to the stimulating of excellence. In talking one day of his college life Phillips Brooks playfully recalled how 'the gigantic mind of President Walker applied itself to determining whether Bill ―― knew his lessons. What Barlow or Paine, our first scholars, knew did not interest the teacher, and we all knew that Bill never knew his lesson.' This situation was unchanged in 1869. 'Gigantic minds' were still preoccupied in disciplining the refractory or indolent. My only permanent reminiscence of Professor Torrey's expositions of history is that he advised us always to read a title page; and of Professor Cooke's instruction in chemistry, that it was indistinguishable from the most exasperating form of mathematics, except by its occasional and malodorous smells.

There were, it may be gratefully added, amid this academic darkness some signs, among those interests which seemed then, as they do to the present generation, to be 'college activities,' that dawn was approaching. In 1866 my big brother rowed in a winning crew at Worcester against Yale, and for the next four years the habit of victory persisted. In 1868 I had the happiness of playing in the first ball game with Yale, and it was won by Harvard in what seems the fantastic score of 25 to 17. How little one realizes at the time when the great moments of his life arrive! One may toil for forty years at his vocation, only to learn that his title to a place in history is derived from an accident which he had quite forgotten. It was only a few years ago that, to my entire surprise, I heard the announcement made at a baseball dinner that I was a living link between the prehistoric and the recorded eras of Harvard athletics, being the first man who ever went to the bat against Yale! For the next five years similar halos crowned Harvard ball-teams, though with a diminishing brilliancy, which prophesied, as in rowing, the characteristic disinclination of Yale to remain defeated. In 1873 a score of 19 to 17 was the omen of disaster, and the bright dawn of victory soon lapsed into a period of athletic gloom.

One fact of physiological interest has been lately called to my attention by an indefatigable historian of sports. It appears that a singular gift of longevity adheres to the position of first-base, which I had the honor, rather incompetently, to hold. Other positions in that antediluvian era have been robbed by death of nearly all their occupants, but there are, I am assured, no less than five first-basemen of that period, now averaging eighty years of age, still playing the game of life, and not yet called home by the indisputable Umpire.

These incidents of academic life sixty years ago lead to a surprising and instructive reminiscence. If any one who was in those remote days a student in Harvard College were now asked to name the personal influence which he still recalls as most beneficent, he would almost inevitably single out, not the most notable scholar of the time, or the most gifted of teachers, or the most eloquent of orators, but the friend and counsellor who, by common consent of that generation, was given the title of the 'College Saint.'

Dr. Peabody, of whom I was in only a very remote degree a family connection, cannot be named in the same category with Agassiz or Gray or Goodwin. His learning was not profound, and had been acquired as a by-product of pastoral life. He wrote copiously, but he wrote nothing that long survived. He was not eloquent as a preacher or inspiring as a teacher. His sermons were devout and gracious, but seldom incisive or stirring, and his instruction in ethics was little more than a hearing of stumbling recitations from a memorized text. My most vivid recollection of his classroom is his conspicuous manner of recording marks. A perfect recitation gained an 8, and the entire class habitually watched with gay scrutiny the top of the doctor's pencil inscribe two connected circles, and applauded their successful classmate with derisive enthusiasm. His habitual demeanor was absent-minded and unobservant, and he was, as Saint Paul said of charity, gentle and easy to be entreated. Clever youths easily persuaded him to believe in their virtues, and even in their intellectual attainments, though these gifts had not been disclosed either to their classmates or to their own consciences. Among the myths which gathered about

his name was that of a student who inquired what
mark he had received in examination, to which the
kindly doctor is said to have replied, 'A very good
mark indeed. By the way, what is your name?'
He was assigned to the paralyzing task of conducting
daily prayers in the dusk of the morning, with a
congregation herded in under the strokes of an irritating bell; and most of that half-clad and drowsy
congregation observed little more than the curious
and still inexplicable fact that the doctor took off
his spectacles to read and put them on to pray.

His tendency to abstraction was forced upon my
attention in an amusing manner on the festal day
when the class of 1869 celebrated its graduation. Being designated as orator of this Class-Day ceremony,
and remembering that it was one of the last occasions
when Dr. Peabody, as acting president, would preside over our affairs, I prepared what seemed to me
an appropriate paragraph of eulogy, and in the best
sophomoric manner turned with a gesture of appreciation to address our beloved friend, only to discover that the warmth of the June day, or of the
orator's eloquence, had lulled the venerable official
into a nap, from which he was abruptly waked by
a bombardment of hilarious applause.

Yet, by a universal consent which reassures one's
confidence in the ruling instincts of healthy-minded
young men, the tradition became fixed, and is still
cherished by the few survivors of that distant era,

that the excellence of gentle courtesy and of consistent piety was chiefly shown them by this unassuming witness of the simplicity which is in Christ. Indeed, they may even conclude in retrospect that the doctor's simplicity was not so unsophisticated as it seemed; that his guilelessness was not inconsistent with shrewdness, and that he was not so blind as he seemed to the faults which he so freely forgave.

Such, with all his obvious limitations, was the friend who for thirty-three years won from Harvard students a veneration denied to many erudite scholars, but gladly rendered to a college saint. It was a striking instance of what the jargon of the psychologists call 'survival value.' Character proved more enduring than genius. Life was the light of men. Tongues shall cease, taught the Apostle Paul, and knowledge shall vanish away; but these three abide, Faith, Hope, and Love, and the greatest of these is Love.

ANDREW PRESTON PEABODY was born in Beverly, Massachusetts, in 1811, and exhibited in his earliest years a precocity which is almost beyond belief. He could read, it is reported, when he was three years old, and having learned his letters from a book held upside down, acquired the extraordinary gift of inverted reading, so that later, as a teacher, he could follow the pupil's textbook over the top of the page. When this infant prodigy was twelve years old he passed with distinction the entrance examinations of Harvard College, but, being not unreasonably regarded as somewhat immature, remained for a year under private instruction. Such detention, however, proved fruitless, for in one year's study he anticipated two years of college work; entered as a junior, and graduated in 1826 at the age of fifteen; being, with the exception of Paul Dudley of the class of 1690, the youngest boy — one is tempted to say, child — that ever received the Harvard degree.

The normal career of a bookish and pious youth of that generation was predetermined. It began with a few years of bread-winning as a school-master; in this case a harrowing experience of imparting knowledge to boys who would not learn, but could easily thrash their half-grown teacher. Being later asked whether he had found pleasure in these years, he replied that he enjoyed the vacations! There followed three years of residence in Cambridge, where the strain of theological study was relaxed by the teaching of Hebrew to undergraduates. In 1833 he was appointed assistant to the venerable pastor of an important church in Portsmouth, New Hampshire; but the senior minister died within a few weeks after the boy's ordination, and the youth of twenty-two years found himself in charge of the parish, and remained its minister for twenty-seven years.

He was a shy and awkward lad, and certain angularities persisted throughout his life, as in the habit,

Andrew Preston Peabody

noted with amusement by college boys, of walking with one foot on the curb and the other in the gutter. He was, however sustained by two endowments, which were not less permanent than his mannerisms, — the undisguised and unmistakable genuineness of his religious life, and a constitutional vitality and endurance which practically freed him from physical limitations and made work a joy. Two sermons on each Sunday and the intervening obligations of a city pastor left him so unexhausted that in 1852 he undertook to edit the 'North American Review,' and contributed articles to almost every number of that important journal; so that his writings filled a total of more than sixteen hundred pages. Twenty years later, when as a young pastor I was finding the conduct of one service of worship a sufficient occupation for Sunday, I was told by Dr. Peabody that he had walked in the early morning from Cambridge to Salem, a matter of some twenty miles, arriving in time to preach there with undiminished vigor.

After this remarkable term of pastoral life, Dr. Peabody was called, in 1860, by Harvard University, to occupy the chair endowed through the will of Miss Caroline Plummer of Salem. It had happened that a leading citizen of that town, Judge White, in an address before the Harvard Alumni, had expressed his concern for the moral security of students, and had said: 'Let the next foundation laid here in aid of education be a professorship of the philosophy of the heart and the moral life.' This sentence attracted the attention of his friend Miss Plummer; and in her will of 1845 she made provision for the support of a 'Professor of the philosophy of the heart, whose province it shall be to instruct the students in what most nearly concerns their moral and physical welfare, their health, their good habits, and their Christian character, acting toward them by personal intercourse and persuasion the part of parent, as well as that of a teacher and friend.' Miss Plummer died in 1854, and in the following year the President and Fellows of the University, apprehensive, not unreasonably, that a 'professorship of the heart' might be interpreted by susceptible boys as proposing a course in pre-nuptial training, determined, after much conference with the executors of Miss Plummer, to free the bequest from its emotional appeal, and to describe it as endowing a 'Professorship of Christian Morals.'

The title is, no doubt, of more scholastic appropriateness; but the phrase of Miss Plummer more accurately represented the character, both of the first appointment, Reverend Frederic Dan Huntington, later the Protestant Episcopal Bishop of Central New York, who served from 1855–60, and of his successor, who for twenty-one years (1860–81), was in fact a professor of the heart. He participated, it is true, in much classroom instruction in logic, ethics, and Hebrew, but was primarily concerned with the conduct of worship and the pastoral care of the unending procession of youth which from year to year entered and departed through the college gates. He was twice designated as Acting President of the University; in 1862, after the death of President Felton, and again in 1868, after the resignation of President Hill.

Judged by later standards of fitness, when the executive officer of a university has to deal with great problems of finance and expansion, no one could seem less qualified for such administration than a professor of the heart. He brought to this office, it is true, a certain shrewdness and tact which reduced the friction of academic life, and an unfailing kindliness which disarmed opposition ; but no propositions of bold initiative or startling reform could be expected from him, and the transition from his tranquillizing influence to the radical modernism of President Eliot was contemplated by many conservative advisers with alarm. It was urged that the University would be safer under the paternal care of Dr. Peabody than under that of a venturesome youth of thirty-five years, who would be likely to exhibit the qualities of a scientific expert, rather than of a Christian pastor. Indeed, this sense of regret survived among some of the Old Guard through many years of the new régime, and was expressed by the sister of an elderly professor, when talking with me of my own sister, who had married young Eliot and had died at the very time when he was elected president. 'It reconciles me,' said the indomitable reactionary, Miss Torrey, 'to the early death of our beloved Ellen, that she should not have to witness what the University has come to in these days.'

However it may have been for the University, it was fortunate for Dr. Peabody that he was permitted to remain a professor of the heart, for this, rather than administrative leadership, was his manifest vocation. He was not inspiring as a classroom teacher. It was a pleasant jest among my classmates to commit to memory a rhetorical passage from his textbook on 'Christianity the Religion of Nature' and recite it to the author, who had forgotten the source but warmly commended the doctrine, amid the ironical applause of the class. Neither could he be described as a great preacher. His gift of composition was so fluent and prolific that the results were more like unstudied conversations than like convincing arguments or profound appeals. It was his not infrequent practice to complete the writing of a sermon at a single sitting, and the results bear the marks of ease and intimacy rather than of studied reasoning. Meeting a friend late on a Saturday evening, he remarked, 'I must go home and prepare my sermon for to-morrow.' His conduct of worship was singularly reverent and restrained, as of one whose religious experience was a natural

and unforced function of life ; his manner of preaching was contemplative and grave, emphasized by a
certain explosiveness of tone at each transition, which
soon subsided into reflective calm. No listener could
fail to realize the elevation and serenity of his mind ;
but the magnetic touch and the thrill of emotion
were not within the range of his tranquil and academic mood.

Nor can it be maintained that Dr. Peabody's
literary work had in it the quality of permanence.
His productiveness was in quantity almost beyond
belief. There are not less than one hundred and
ninety titles of his writings in the catalogue of the
University library, and in the last twenty years of
his life he published one hundred and twenty books
or pamphlets, so that he was justified in saying that
he felt 'lost' if no proof-sheets were passing through
his hands. Lowell lectures, theological treatises,
journals of travel, translations of Cicero and
Plutarch, and volumes of sermons, were interspersed
with occasional addresses at colleges, town celebrations, ordinations, and anniversaries ; and this mass of
material, none of it hasty or trivial, was produced with
none of the modern devices of stenography or type-
writing, but by the unremitting toil of his own hand.

It sometimes happens that a man of letters has to
make a deliberate choice between the ephemeral
service of his own generation and the detached and
concentrated devotion to a masterpiece ; as when

Macaulay withdrew from the House of Commons to write the 'History of England,' surrendering, as his biographer has said, 'more than most men could hope to win.' More frequently, however, this dissipation of energy is forced on one by circumstances, and as one yields himself to incidental claims he may be consoled by reflecting that the *magnum opus* of which he has dreamed might perhaps in any event have remained unwritten, or — worse — unread. Dr. Peabody's lavish use of his literary gifts was a part of his characteristic generosity. He was capable of productions which might endure, being cultivated in the classics, lecturing at short notice on Plato and Aristotle and writing of Plutarch; but the calls constantly made on him for counsel or commemoration commanded his willing response, and his literary monument is to be found in the lives which he reënforced and the occasions which he adorned.

These limitations, however, only make the nature of his influence the more remarkable. Hearers might listen to his sermons with respect but without enthusiasm, and readers might find in his writings judicious reflections rather than comprehensive mastery; but there was no resisting the extraordinary — indeed, almost unique — impression of a benignant and beneficent character, which in the minds of college youth made even eccentricity of manner endearing, and soon became a precious tradition of university life. 'I like to see his light burning as I pass his house,' said one undergraduate, who had perhaps never entered the home or spoken to its occupant, 'and know that the old man is there.'

Never were this serenity and simplicity of character more impressive than in Dr. Peabody's last years. It is no slight strain on temper and patience to withdraw from active service while still vigorous in mind and body, and to have the work to which one has given himself taken over by a young and untried successor. Yet this transition was made, not with resignation, but with parental coöperation and confidence. The inclination to conservatism which had marked Dr. Peabody's life was wholly subordinated to the hope of a larger service, in which he was not to share, but to which he gave his gracious benediction. He died in 1893, at the age of eighty-two, leaving, as the Apostle Eliot said of one of his contemporaries, 'a good savour.'

The impression made by his conduct of morning prayers is perhaps sufficiently indicated by these lines of playful reminiscence:

'See, then, each day reluctantly begin
With grudging praise and pious discipline;
Let the bell's clangor rend the morning air
And summon drowsy boys to early prayer;
Let docile youth be trained to kiss the rod
And learn by chastisement the love of God;
Let their prompt rising shame the laggard sun,
And those who hope to pray first learn to run.
In vain this penal pietism strives
To wake devotion within dormant lives;

Present-Day Saints

In vain the breathless, half-clad youngsters come
To dedicate their day's curriculum ;
In vain the meagre praise and tuneless hymn,
The hastening fugue and halting cherubim ;
In vain the proctors watch from high settees,
While keen-eyed monitors prick absentees.
No languid reverence for a sacred past
Can satisfy the young iconoclast ;
No peremptory prayer his soul confine,
No ancient bottle hold youth's foaming wine.
Yet in that dreary dawn and wintry chill,
One gracious figure warms the memory still ;
Devout, benignant, and serenely kind,
His prayer the gesture of his humble mind,
With no parade of homiletic art,
He thawed the chapel by sheer warmth of heart ;
Hushing the restless throng with gracious tone,
And all unconscious that his visage shone,
In the dim pulpit, homely, ruddy, quaint,
He stood, the student's friend and college saint.'

A more adequate appreciation of his life is engraved
on a tablet set near the pulpit where his benignant
presence had been so long familiar :

ANDREW PRESTON PEABODY, D.D., LL.D.
Plummer Professor of Christian Morals and Preacher to the
University

Born at Beverly, March 19, 1811
Died at Cambridge, March 10, 1893.
Author, Editor, Teacher, Preacher, Helper of Men
Three generations looked to him
As to a Benefactor, a Friend, a Father
His Precept was Glorified by His Example
While for Thirty-Three Years
He moved among the Teachers and Students of
Harvard College
And Wist not that His Face Shone

CHAPTER III

JAMES FREEMAN CLARKE

AN impression often entertained of college boys is that they are completely absorbed in frivolous self-indulgence diversified by a passionate love of sport, and are for the time being quite impervious to serious interests of life or faith. A Harvard professor, esteemed by his fellows as peculiarly sagacious, remarked, when it was proposed to abandon compulsion in worship and offer religion to Harvard students as a privilege, that the plan was sure to fail, because college boys were at precisely that point in life when the inhibitions of their homes were outgrown, and no other spiritual motive had been reached. They were lusty young animals, who must wait for the chastening experiences of mature life to humanize them.

No estimate of the normal state of intelligent youth between seventeen and twenty years of age could be more inadequate. Many of them, it is true, either because of an injudicious selection of their parents, or because of the excessive paternalism of their schools, or through the force of unregulated passions in their own emotional life, become self-indulgent, irresponsible, or animalized; but with great numbers of youths of that age there is an emergence of moral restlessness, an apologetic interest in doing good, a secret thirst for God, a kind of spiritual chastity which dreads exposure and would rather be mistaken for indifference than discovered to be serious-mindedness or piety. Such boys may even welcome surreptitious ways of self-expression lest they be detected in doing good and forfeit their standing as men of the world.

The same phenomenon is often met in a young man's intellectual life. The latter half of his college course is for many youths a time of clarifying intention, which is like one's first glimpse of land after a long voyage at sea. The distant outlines of a vocation may be at first hardly distinguishable from cloud-land, but by degrees they become defined and substantial, and even suggest a harbor. The boy says to himself: 'I will at least steer toward the study of medicine'; 'I will try the road to the law.' Then what has seemed purposeless routine, the first principle of which was avoidance of penalties or success in the game of student versus teacher, is touched with a zest and joy which surprise both the youth and the faculty. The idler finds himself a worker. A sense of direction is given him, as though he saw a lighthouse through the mist and could steer straight for a port. Only one condition limits this increasing sense of certainty: it must be for the present a secret possession. The youth still cherishes his good name as an amateur or a sport. He must be free to shift his course; there are other harbors on the map;

James Freeman Clarke

what seems a vision may turn out to be a mirage. Such, I have learned from long observation of youth, is a common, if not a normal, condition of emerging manhood, the birth of a mind, the sighting of a new continent within reach even of a boy's self-distrust.

What curious, and as it might seem trivial, incidents give intimation of this approach to reality, as a land breeze, with its savor of pines, steals out into the sea! I recall, for example, an audacious adventure made late in my sophomore year. Having casually heard of an obscure evangelical work in Boston called the North End Mission, my college-mate Van Rensselaer Thayer and I slipped away from our homes on a Sunday afternoon and stole down from Beacon Hill, as if on some nefarious errand, to the Bad Lands of Salem Street, enlisting there as teachers, where no one knew our names or qualifications — still less our completely inadequate theology. Neither of us knew what orthodoxy meant or had the least equipment for biblical teaching. It was not long before the discerning boys of the North End discovered such 'easy marks,' and appeared in shoes which so eloquently pleaded for renewal that we lined up our protégées on Monday at the only shop where we were at home, and, to the bewilderment of the excellent Mr. Rogers, fitted new shoes over ragged stockings and sent our pupils limping away. There never was a more impotent attempt at Christianization; but it may at least have brought some mercenary benefit to the North End; for such of the boys as appeared for instruction the next Sunday were shod in nothing stiffer than what the Apostle called 'the preparation of the gospel of peace.'

In later life, when it was my privilege to advise college boys, I had many occasions to observe the same moral diffidence and spiritual secretiveness. It would seem not unlike the inclination which, it is said, sometimes leads a Roman Catholic penitent to resort to a stranger rather than to his own parish priest, so that confession shall be completely impersonal and anonymous. Many years ago, for instance, I was watching one day the swirl and drive of a violent blizzard when there entered my study an unknown student, wrapped in one ulster and carrying another. Without giving his name he said that as he was sitting at the window of his club it occurred to him that his second coat might be of use to some other man in such a storm, and, not having any acquaintance with needy students, he had brought it to me to give away. Nothing would have offended this young benefactor more seriously than to be charged by his fellows with philanthropic sentimentalism. Both of his ulsters were obviously from London, and it was from the window of our least ascetic club that he had watched the storm. Yet the gale without had roused him from satiety within, and the sudden impulse of kindliness which he had experienced demanded only that it should not be found out. What immediately followed was still more surprising. By one of those coincidences which seem foreordained, this youth had hardly plunged out into the drifts when another student, ill-clad and chilled, appeared, hoping that the ill-wind of the storm might blow him some good in the form of work; and soon this second visitor withdrew, with every external sign of being a gentleman of leisure, robed in an ulster cut by Poole.

Under the Harvard system of a staff of preachers, the minister conducting daily prayers spends two hours of each morning during his term of service in the Preachers' Room, to welcome there any student who may wish to consult him; and these hours in what may be fairly called a confessional have abounded in evidences of the same shy but compelling altruism. A young man, for instance, enters in an obviously emotional agitation, and says abruptly, 'Can you tell me, Sir, where I can find work in a boys' club?' and the preacher, realizing that there is something behind this apparently unprovoked desire, asks, 'Why do you wish to add this social service to the work of your busy winter?' 'Well, the fact is,' answers the inquirer, 'that I find my life very empty and tempted this winter, and I thought I should like to do something for somebody else.' It was the shy and undefined response of the boy's soul to the call of God; the resurgence of the spirit through the solicitations of the flesh; the modern, though unspoken, reiteration of the cry of Saint Augustine, 'My heart is restless until it finds rest in Thee.'

Such, I am led to believe, is a normal experience of maturing manhood, unless it be choked by the deceitfulness of riches or the lust of other things; and as I look back on the first boyish adventures of my own religious interest I see that they were not so much daring as inevitable; the timid ventures of the spirit into an unexplored universe. I had been bred in the decorum and restraint of King's Chapel, where worship was reverent and stately, and emotionalism inappropriate or unknown; and when in my senior year in college the germs of the religious life began to fructify my first impulse was to run away from the risks of kindly scrutiny, and to look for guidance where I was not known. It happened that in the South End of Boston — a region practically unexplored by worshippers at King's Chapel — a friend of my father's had established a new kind of church, frequented by what to me was a new kind of people. The minister was, I knew, a scholar; but he was also an unconventional and unecclesiastical reformer, who had gathered round him a constituency of minds like his own and formed what was more like a family than a church. No hiding-place could be safer from discovery by the reverent and contented congregation of King's

James Freeman Clarke

Chapel, and, with the exhilaration of escape and the confidence of solitude I ventured into the uncharted wilderness of the South End, and sought the teaching of James Freeman Clarke.

There were, it is true, some points of contact which encouraged this migration. Dr. Clarke had been himself a child of King's Chapel, being the step-grandchild of James Freeman, the daring revisionist of the King's Chapel liturgy. He had been, as I was, baptized at the chancel of that venerable church. He had been a colleague of my father in missionary adventures in the Middle West; and this companionship had led my father to name one of his daughters after Dr. Clarke's lovely wife. Yet it was not propinquity which persuaded me, but remoteness. The first condition of religious interest was that it should not be expressed under the scrutiny, still less with the affectionate stimulation, of family or friends.

It happened that at just this time scholars were becoming aware of the dignity and beauty of religions beyond the area of the Christian tradition, and there were premonitions of the new science of Comparative Religion, which reached its first conspicuous expression in Max Müller's edition of the 'Sacred Books of the East,' published in 1879. The venturesome mind of the minister at the South End was among the first to appreciate the significance of this expansion of spiritual sympathy, and he at once applied himself to study the great religions of the world. On the way to this laborious undertaking, he proposed to his young parishoners a plan of study, unique, so far as I know, among the churches of that time. To each member of his class was assigned one of the world-religions, with such references as could be named for guidance from books ; and on successive Sundays this student was to report the teaching of his selected faith concerning God, man, duty, immortality, and other cardinal themes. The teacher, thereupon, at each session, summarized and synthesized the subject in its Christian aspect.

Thus, however crude or inconclusive the inquiries of students might be, they were a suggestion of what is now called the 'case-system,' which has become the ruling method of the higher education, and they were probably one of the earliest explorations made by American students in the unmapped regions of comparative religion. These discussions were sifted and clarified by Dr. Clarke during the next year, and made the basis of the volume known as 'Ten Great Religions,' which was published in 1871, and which, though inevitably superseded in large part by more erudite works, still remains not only readable but prophetic. That an active pastor, at a time when the study of ethnic religions was just emerging from prevailing ignorance and prejudice, should have foreseen the priceless contributions to Christian faith soon to be made, was of itself enough to give distinction to any scholar. I attached myself with enthusiasm to this group of young men, all strangers to me, and none of them of college connection, but contributing by their business experience and knowledge of the world, not only to what Dr. Clarke called 'common sense in religion,' but also to the great enlightenment of the one member of the class who had fancied that Harvard College possessed the secret of a liberal education.

Little did I dream that the father-confessor, thus sought because he was a stranger, would come to be the most trusted of counsellors, and would hold for me throughout his life a unique place of sane and far-sighted leadership. Still less did I know that, by a happy coincidence, Dr. Clarke's home was in the immediate neighborhood of the family where four years later I was to find my wife, and that this counsellor of my religious life had been for years the playful companion of a daughter of the house. As a natural consequence of these varied associations, which drew me as by spiritual attraction toward this commanding personality, Dr. Clarke married me to his young playmate in 1872; in 1874 participated in my ordination to the ministry; and remained until his death, in 1878, the most benignant of friends.

JAMES FREEMAN CLARKE was born in 1810; passed his boyhood in the home of Dr. Freeman, for whom he was named; graduated from Harvard College in 1829 at the age of nineteen; and after studying at the Harvard Divinity School pushed out into what was then the remote region of Kentucky, and became, when but twenty-three years old, a pastor in Louisville. He had been bred in the anti-slavery circle of Boston and the Puritan ethics of Massachusetts, and he now found himself among slave-holders and defenders of the duel; but his gentle candor and consistent honesty disarmed serious opposition. His notes on this experience indicate the conflicting impressions which he received from this novel environment: 'Very green and raw when I reached Louisville.' 'Character of people manly, intelligent, generous, fresh.' 'Judge Rowan, eminent lawyer, Senator of the United States, courteous, gallant, and scholarly, has fought at least one duel.' 'George D. Prentice. His wife's party. I refused wine. He asked why.' 'Mr. Prentice has offered Mr. Trotter to fight with rifles at forty-five paces, or with pistols at six, or with swords or dirks. Then it was said that Mr. Trotter had demanded on account of his nearsightedness to fight with pistols at each other's breasts; and then the negotiations broke off.' 'Every day I become more interested in the character of this great Western people. Its simplicity charms me; its openness commands my sympathy; its free, unfettered activity calls for my admiration.'

James Freeman Clarke

The most notable incident of this missionary service was the establishing and maintaining, with his
two friends, Ephraim Peabody in Cincinnati and
William G. Eliot in St. Louis, the journal called 'The
Western Messenger,' which in its six years of publication (1835–41) was an organ not only of theological
liberalism but also of distinguished literary contributions. Young Clarke was an eager student of the
German poets, then strangers to most Americans,
and he translated and published passages from
Goethe and Schiller. Ralph Waldo Emerson sent
him many poems, including 'Each and All,' 'The
Humble Bee,' and 'The Rhodora,' appending to
the last the comment, 'You are quite welcome to
the lines "To the Rhodora," but I think they need
the superscription "Lines on being asked 'Whence
is the flower?'".' In 1839 Clarke writes to Emerson
one of many acknowledgments, 'I received your kind
letter including the lines "Good-bye, proud world,"
for which I thank you.'

The most interesting of all these notable contributions was a considerable series received from no
less a person than John Keats, whose brother Thomas
had settled in Louisville, and through whom were
obtained for 'The Western Messenger' a letter from
the poet to his brother with verses inspired by Fin-
gal's Cave, extracts from a journal written by John
Keats when but twenty-two years of age during a
pedestrian tour, and describing Winander Lake and

Ambleside Fall; and, most important of all, the lovely 'Hymn to Apollo' beginning:

> 'God of the golden bow,
> And of the golden lyre,
> And of the golden hair,
> And of the golden fire,
> Charioteer
> Of the patient year.'

An obscure denominational paper published in Kentucky which could prefix to this contribution the note, 'The following beautiful poem is for the first time published from the original manuscript, presented to the editor by the poet's brother,' deserves for this alone a place in literary history.

After eight years of this brave venture, the young minister was urged to return to Boston, where, as Dr. Channing wrote, the preaching had become 'lacking in authority and life' and needed 'your bolder tone, your firmer faith.' This bolder tone and firmer faith made Clarke an innovator in Boston, as they had made him a radical in Louisville. The churches with which he became associated, and at their head the King's Chapel of his boyhood, were fast anchored in the proprietary system, under which pew-holders were occupants of their own estates, and had the right to be undisturbed in their favorite corners or their habits of somnolence by the invasion of casual worshippers. Indeed, there still remains in King's Chapel at least one family pew the title-deed of which stands in the name of an ancestor who was a college mate of Dr. Freeman in 1777.

The invader of this stronghold of ecclesiastical capitalism had the audacity to propose 'not a congregation of Unitarians but a Church of Christ.' It should be 'built on coincidence of practical purpose. Those who intend to do the same things will unite in it. All who join this church dedicate themselves with all the faculties of mind and body to the service of Jesus Christ.' In a word, it was to be true to the name selected for its organization, 'The Church of the Disciples.' Such a scheme, involving the abandonment of a pew-holding body or an annual tax, and complete freedom of seating and payment, was a type of organization now familiar but then revolutionary, and drew to its unqualified congregationalism so many young and venturesome spirits that one neighboring minister playfully said of Dr. Clarke, 'He is nothing but a thief and a robber.' Other churches of Boston were largely local in their constituency, but the new organization gathered its congregation from such scattered and even remote districts that it became known as 'The Church of the Carry-alls.'

This novel enterprise held its meetings for worship, first in a little chapel which Beacon Street carried, as it were, in a pocket known as Freeman Place, later in a region remote from Beacon Hill and uncharted on the map of society, called Indiana Place, and finally in a building not easily distinguished from a gasometer in the still less explored jungle of Warren Avenue. To a boy who had been bred in the dignified worship of King's Chapel, the conversational piety of this unqualified democracy could but seem lacking in decorum and æsthetic effect; but there was a fraternal simplicity which gave religion fresh reality and comprehensiveness. What the new church lacked in dignity it atoned for by reality. It was unadorned but wide-awake. Its minister soon testified that he recognized no limitation of sect or form; for he exchanged with Theodore Parker on the one hand, and with Dr. Kirk, the pillar of Boston orthodoxy, on the other; and he baptized by immersion whenever that primitive rite was desired. In a word, the new congregation was not a passive audience, but a coöperative household.

In the charming romance of Sir Thomas More, written more than four hundred years ago, he pictures a cheerful communism in which, as he says, 'The whole land is, as it were, one family'; but he is forced to conclude of this Utopian Commonwealth, 'I must needs confess and grant that many things be in the Utopian Weal Publick which in other cities I may rather wish for than hope after.' A similar impression of an ecclesiastical Utopia was made on a child of King's Chapel by the Church of the Disciples. The whole company was, as it were, one family — a realization of primitive Christianity which in other churches was rather wished for than hoped after.

A noble and diversified company found this domestic fellowship congenial and reassuring. John Albion Andrew, later the War Governor of Massachusetts, was one of its first adherents, and said of it: 'I do not know how I could overestimate the influence of this Home of the Soul on the happiness and welfare of my life, . . . its creed as comprehensive as the formulary of the first Apostles, its spirit of brotherhood as expansive as the charity of the Christian faith.' Julia Ward Howe was through all her later life a devoted member of what she described as 'a living church built out of his [Dr. Clarke's] own devout and tender heart.' Oliver Wendell Holmes, though remaining loyal to his own religious home at King's Chapel, and often, as I can testify from personal observation, tranquilly slumbering in his corner of the gallery, wrote with balanced judgment of his neighbor:

> 'True to all truth the world denies,
>   Not tongue-tied for its gilded sin;
>   Not always right in all men's eyes,
>   But faithful to the light within.'

In his 'Professor at the Breakfast Table' he describes, under the thin disguise of 'The Church of the Galileans,' the work and atmosphere of the Church of the Disciples. 'How different it was,' he says, 'from the Church of Saint Polycarp! No clerical costume, no ceremonial forms, no carefully trained choir! . . . These brethren and sisters meet very much as a family does for its devotions, not putting off their humanity in the least, but considering it on the whole quite a delightful matter to come together for prayer and song and good counsel from kind and wise lips.'

Sustained by this intimate fellowship with a few distinguished friends and many less conspicuous lives, James Freeman Clarke at thirty-one years of age began, in 1841, his remarkable career of public service and productive scholarship in Boston. It was a time when the teachings of Channing and Emerson were still dominating the thought of the city and had drawn to its pulpits a group of notable ministers. Among them young Clarke was soon recognized as the most sagacious and consistent. His intellectual productiveness was unremitting, and in every instance was directed, not to maintain a controversy but to analyze and estimate various aspects of truth. His 'Steps of Belief,' 'Essentials and Non-Essentials,' and 'Orthodoxy, its Truth and Errors,' illustrate this temperamental tolerance; and his 'Ideas of Paul,' 'Events and Epochs of Christian History,' and 'Problems of the Four Gospels' have the same marks of poise and discernment. It was this quality of sanity in judgment which made him, more than any other man of his generation, the typical representative of Liberal Christianity — liberal because trained to appreciate the catholicity of truth. 'The lines which unite Christians,' he said, 'are not theological parallels of latitude, but the isothermal lines of faith. I often find myself in the same religious climate, on the same isothermal line, with men from whom I differ very widely in my religious creed.' It was a faith which was liberal, not because it was loose or indifferent, but because it was discerning and catholic. 'The Church,' he wrote, 'is the body of Christ — an organization through which the spirit of Christ can work. . . . Faith leads to work; work also leads to faith. He who does a great Christian work casts himself on God for strength. Our working men should also be praying men.'

Even more prophetic of the future was the programme proposed by Dr. Clarke for theological education. He was four times elected as an Overseer of Harvard College, and for several years lectured in its Divinity School; and this association led him to reconsider the organization of professional study and to propose what he called a 'University of Theology.' It should not ignore or depreciate denominational differences but should 'extend to the Department of Theology the system of University lectures already inaugurated in other Departments' and 'invite eminent men from every school of opinion to give courses of lectures on some branch of theology,' so that there should be 'one school of Christian theology where the student can hear differing and opposing views calmly and honestly stated.' It was an ideal which anticipated by more than twenty years the programme boldly undertaken by President Eliot, and which has now become in large part realized, both by the composition of the Harvard Faculty of Theology, and by the affiliation of its school with those in its neighborhood controlled by various denominations.

These and many other undertakings of religious and theological activity would seem enough to fill the busy days of a parish minister, but they represent in fact only the inner circle of Dr. Clarke's versatile productiveness. The whole range of contemporary politics, literature, and science was within his province. Nothing human was foreign to him. He was thrown into the full stream of the anti-slavery agitation, and had the great advantage of seeing the institution of slavery at its best, as well as at its worst, during his residence in Kentucky. 'I learned my anti-slavery lessons,' he said, 'from slavery itself and from the slave-holders round me.' While he resolutely maintained that 'slavery must be destroyed or it will destroy us,' and personally wrote the protest signed by one hundred and seventy-three Unitarian ministers, who pledged themselves 'before God and our brethren never to be weary of laboring in the cause of human rights and freedom till slavery

James Freeman Clarke

be abolished and every slave made free,' he did not
associate himself with the aggressive programme of
the Anti-Slavery Society, and was regarded by its
extreme representatives as lukewarm, when he was
in fact far-sighted and sane. He wrote history and
biography — 'History of the Campaign of 1812'
(1884); 'Anti-Slavery Days' (1886); he translated
from the German Hase's 'Life of Jesus' (1860); he
collected his own versified translations from various
sources in 'Exotics' (1876). Among other avocations
of his tireless mind he became an expert astronomer,
inventing an 'Astronomical Atlas' and describing it
in a little book, 'How to Find the Stars' (1878).
Woman's suffrage, the education of women, the peace
movement, prison reform — all these aspects of the
new humanism of his time found in him a gallant
defender. His list of publications numbers thirty
volumes, besides an almost countless number of
periodical contributions.

Such prodigious versatility would have betrayed
many a man into intellectual instability, where
sympathy outran knowledge and influence was lost
by intellectual dissipation. Nothing, however, was
more remote from Dr. Clarke's temperament than
such divisive superficiality. These varied interests
were the sheer overflow of his intellectual vitality,
and reënforced his primary function of the ministry,
as little streams swell the abundance of a river. His
diversified appreciation commended him to many

minds which would not listen to the ordinary preacher; for he impressed them as a reformer without obsessions, a controversialist who could be just, and a saint who could be playful. Dr. Samuel G. Howe, the most distinguished figure in American philanthropy, and a member of Dr. Clarke's congregation, in a letter to his friend Theodore Parker, ventured to dwell on the besetting fault of that remarkable man. 'Dear Parker,' wrote Howe, 'you overrate things. You are childish about some matters of common sense. You are encouraged to be thinking and saying sharp and cutting things. God bless you, dear Parker, and before you meet Him face to face may some spots of hard grit be removed from your warm and loving heart.' Dr. Howe would have used no such words if he had been writing of his pastor, whom his family called 'Our dear Saint James.' There was no hard grit rasping Dr. Clarke's heart, no overrating of issues, no sharp and cutting way of saying things. Scrupulous justice to the opponent's position, a clearer exposition of evangelical teaching than its own expounders could offer — these qualities commended to thousands his 'Orthodoxy, its Truths and Errors' and his 'Steps to Belief,' and the reader felt himself led up these successive steps as if holding a firm hand.

This confidence in his judicial temper and unclouded insight made him a trusted adviser even in commercial or political affairs, and, in one instance, in the critical issues of a heated presidential campaign. Dr. Clarke had been for many years associated with the Republican party; but, with many of its supporters, in 1884 found himself unable to approve of its candidate, whose fatal letter concerning a certain financial negotiation Dr. Clarke had actually seen, and, indeed, was later able to add to his collection of autographs, where it still exists, with its incriminating postscript, 'Burn this letter.' In the case of the Democratic candidate, Grover Cleveland, though he had been singularly unblemished in his political record, there was much hostile gossip concerning his private character; and Dr. Clarke, like many other voters, seemed to be forced to choose between an unscrupulous politician and a man whose morality was questioned. In this dilemma, Dr. Clarke, without consultation with party leaders or any official authorization, took the train for Albany, conferred at length with Mr. Cleveland, and, returning to Boston, announced his conclusion that conscientious voters would be justified in assuming the essential integrity of the Democratic candidate. It would be extravagant to say that this moral support of an individual was responsible for Mr. Cleveland's election; but it is quite certain that while one precipitate blunder of another minister, concerning 'Rum, Romanism, and Rebellion' cost Mr. Blaine great numbers of votes, the judicial statement of Dr. Clarke became an important factor in securing for the country the brave and magnanimous administration of Mr. Cleveland.

Finally, among these reminiscences of diversified service, it must be once more recalled that all these activities in academic, literary, and political life had their roots deeply set in the immediate duties of a Christian pastor. He could reach out with confidence into social or theological reforms because he stood firmly in his chosen place and commanded the confidence and love of his people. His versatility was not a dissipation of power, but its radiation. He was not what is called an orator, with the passionate appeal of Phillips or the gift for invective of Parker; but he read the future more accurately than either of these, and declined to identify political differences with moral obliquity. His speech was somewhat slow and grave, though with an occasional flash of fire or wit, and his power in public address proceeded from the impression of sagacity, knowledge of the world and of the human heart, and an obvious occupation of his mind with generous thoughts and aims. The studies which might have diverted him from his preaching entered into the fabric of his sermons and gave them stability and authority. Thus in preaching of the leadership of Jesus, he utilized the substance of his 'Ten Great Religions.' 'That which makes the impassable gulf between Jesus and the other great teachers of mankind is his entire confidence in God as his Father and Friend. No one else

among the masters of human thought has shared
it with him. Neither Socrates nor Confucius, neither
Buddha nor Plato, neither Zoroaster nor Moses ever
said " I and my Father are one." . . . It was this
perfect union of his heart, mind, will, with the heart,
mind, and will of God which has made Jesus the
incomparable leader of the human race.'

The physical appearance of Dr. Clarke expressed
his character — the sturdy form, the head bowed by
the scholar's habit of life, the manner weighted by
thought, but roused in utterance to irony or wit.
It was no wonder that a college boy found in such a
teacher the guidance and reassurance he desired. It
must have been much the same with young men who
listened to that disciple of Jesus who was in the same
way both a liberally educated gentleman and a tireless missionary of Christ. The Apostle Paul could
write of the mysteries of Christ in words so subtle
and profound that, as was said of them, there were
'some things hard to be understood, which they that
are unlearned and unstable wrest . . . unto their
own destruction'; but when, the Apostle himself
sums up his counsel to the cultivated Romans he
beseeches them, 'by the mercies of God,' to present
their bodies a 'living sacrifice' which is their 'reasonable service,' or, as the words may be more accurately
rendered, their 'logical sacrifice.' No offering to God
is more essential, now or then, than such a union of
reasonableness and service, of logic and sacrifice.

Present-Day Saints

Much reasoning, now as in Paul's time, is unserviceable, and much service is unreasonable. Much logic is inapplicable to life, and much of life is precipitate and illogical. The Christian apostle, be he named Paul of Tarsus or James of Boston, who can apply the life of reason to the world of service, and direct service by a reasonable mind, is a guide to whom loyal youth will gladly turn, and who will be tenderly and loyally remembered by them all their days.

They will concur in the convincing testimony offered in Trinity Church by Phillips Brooks on the Sunday after the death of his neighbor and friend: 'He belonged to the whole Church of Christ. Through him his Master spoke to all who had ears to hear. Especially, he was a living, perpetual epistle to the Church of God which is in Boston. It is a beautiful, a solemn moment, when the City, the Church, and the World, gather up the completeness of a finished life like his and thank God for it, and place it in the shrine of memory to be a power and a revelation thenceforth so long as City and Church and World shall last. It is not the losing, it is rather the gaining, the assuring of his life — whatever he has gone to in the great mystery beyond, he remains a word of God here in the world he loved. Let us thank our heavenly Father for the life, the work, the inspiration, of his true servant, his true saint, James Freeman Clarke.'

CHAPTER IV

FRIEDRICH AUGUST GOTTREU THOLUCK

IN June, 1872, I had completed the prescribed course of theological study in the Harvard Divinity School and had received its degree. It had been a disheartening experience of uninspiring study and retarded thought. The fresh breeze of modern thought rarely penetrated the lecture-rooms, and a student found the intellectual atmosphere unexhilarating to breathe. One half of the first year was devoted to the rudiments of the Hebrew language, at the end of which linguistic discipline one could, with the English text well in mind, stumblingly translate the first chapter of Genesis and the twenty-third Psalm; an achievement soon recognized as not contributing materially to the equipment of a modern minister, and therefore promptly forgotten. The Old and New Testaments were presented as material for textual analysis rather than for spiritual inspiration; and theology and ethics were subjects of ecclesiastical erudition and doctrinal desiccation. Now and then the windows were opened to let in the fresh air of teaching by visiting professors; but the only instruction I can recall with positive gratitude was a brief series of familiar talks on the practical duties of the pastor's life, given by a newly appointed professor, who had so lately transferred himself

from the pastorate to academic life that he had not
lost the human touch or the poetic mood. In a word,
education for a profession was in its method and
aims not essentially different from the pedagogical
plan of an elementary school.

A little Polish girl in a New York public school
was asked to write an answer to the question, 'What
is the difference between an educated man and an
intelligent man?' and replied, 'An educated man
knows what other people think, but an intelligent
man works his own thinks.' The same distinction
might be observed in many professional schools
sixty years ago. A student might become educated
while he might remain unintelligent. He might be
able to pass examinations on the thoughts of others
without having any thoughts of his own. I cannot
remember attaining in seven years of Harvard classrooms anything that could be fairly described as an
idea. As an undergraduate the only approach to
thinking that I recall was in the room of a kindly
professor, who was good enough to read Browning
to me after dinner, and to stir my mind by the
teaching of spiritual optimism. The only provoca-
tion to thought which I recall during my theological
course was at a boarding-house, where a robust
materialist and a confirmed sceptic amused themselves at the dinner-table by chaffing the young
theologue about his belated piety and forcing him to
offer retaliatory but unconvincing arguments.

Thr A Tholuck.

Friedrich August Gottreu Tholuck

I vividly remember the precise spot where I was literally struck by something which had the force of an idea. It was in a bookseller's shop in Germany, where I found lying on the counter the two volumes of Pfleiderer's book, just issued — and his first considerable publication — on 'Religion, Its Nature and Its History' (1872). 'There,' I said to myself, 'is what I have been feeling after as the work I should like to do. If one might in any degree rescue religion from provincialism, and verify its philosophy by its history, that would be a task which would challenge a modern man.' It was a vision dimly seen, and later incompletely fulfilled in my first course of lectures at the Harvard Divinity School on the Philosophy of Religion, and in my first articles of any serious intention, on the 'History of the Psychology of Religion' ('Unitarian Review,' 1880, 1883), in both of which the marks of Pfleiderer's influence were conspicuous. It was a peculiar happiness thirty-three years later to be welcomed as a colleague in Berlin by that rugged veteran and untiring controversialist and to report to him the initial momentum which he had given to a dormant mind.

After winning, by sedulous and docile attentiveness, the divinity degree — and indeed before Commencement Day of 1872 — I married, and set forth with my wife into the unknown regions of German theology; being in some degree provoked to this adventure by the irritating practice of one professor in the Harvard School, who insisted on citing German authorities as though they were completely conclusive. 'On this point,' he would say, 'Rothe's view is, as follows,' and would then proceed without further discussion to quote the oracle.

It seemed essential to peace of mind that one should determine whether the gods of German theology were infallible, or whether they might sometimes nod; and I ventured, with a meagre equipment of language, to scale those Olympian heights. The daughter of a Harvard professor of an earlier generation, John Gorham Palfrey — herself a highly cultivated woman — began the study of Hebrew when she was seventy years old, and when asked to defend this enterprise said that as she was soon to meet her Maker she wanted to address Him in his own language. Even this linguistic preparation had been unattained under the method of our Divinity School; and as for German, I recall with still surviving humiliation my reply to the Rector of the University of Halle, who kindly inquired about my father's occupation. I intended to say that he was no longer living ('*Er lebt nicht mehr*'), but in the embarrassment of this interview with an academic dignitary, I answered that he was not yet living ('*Er lebt noch nicht*'); thus suggesting a problem of parentage which must have made American manners and customs more perplexing than ever to the German mind.

Friedrich August Gottreu Tholuck

I had planned to enroll myself at Heidelberg; but a survey of the offerings for the winter semester, and a rather chilling reception by the distinguished Professor Schenkel, drove me to Leipzig. There I found the prevailing attitude of defensive orthodoxy even more repelling than the arid rationalism of Heidelberg. Finally, I fell in behind the long procession of American students who had found at Halle a mediating theology, represented for forty years by the erudite and saintly Professor Tholuck. He was well known to be a lecturer who was at the same time a fervent pietist and an accessible friend of students. To him had come such pupils as Professor Hodge of Princeton and Professor H. B. Smith of Union Seminary. Professor Schaff had been his private secretary. Piety and learning were so intimately blended in his teaching that he had become an object of peculiar affection to those who followed him, and of unsparing criticism from those who regarded this fusion of traits as unscholarly mysticism. His name had become so familiar in academic life that a letter addressed from America to 'Professor Tholuck, Europe,' was, it is said, delivered at his modest home in Halle. With a trembling hand, therefore, I rang his doorbell, and in halting German inquired if the professor were at home. The maid replied with a copious vocabulary which I imperfectly understood, but at least realized was not of marked cordiality, and which indicated that I should have inquired, not for the professor, but for the *Obercousistorialrat.* So resounding a title suggested an imposing personality, but I was soon relieved, in answering his friendly summons to visit him, to find a gentle little man, with entire command of English, and with the kindly manner of a pastor greeting a new member of his flock.

The young American couple, thus settled in a completely strange environment, were soon accepted by the professor and his gracious wife as in some sense their wards; and in the joys and sorrows which were experienced during the following months these kindly and devoted friends became the chief support and resource of a long northern winter in the dullest of German towns.

As a final evidence of paternal affection, Professor Tholuck proposed to read with me, in the privacy of his study, the 'Discourses on Religion' of Schleiermacher, and appointed an hour for our first session. On reaching his home, however, I was met by the sad news that he had either stumbled, or had some strange seizure, on his stairway, and was much shaken both in mind and body. From that time, though he continued to lecture almost until his death in 1877, it was with a broken mind in an enfeebled body, and he was listened to by a diminishing audience, with reverent piety rather than with scholastic enthusiasm. I had therefore the pathetic experience of being the last in the long line

Friedrich August Gottreu Tholuck

of American students who were admitted to his intimacy, and who had the privilege of learning from his life and teaching that the career of a scholar might be consistent with the character of a saint.

I cannot dismiss these reminiscences of student life in Germany without reflecting on the unanticipated and tortuous way along which one's life is often guided through the years. The winter of 1870–71 in Halle was at the time far from exhilarating. A strain of my eyesight made reading impossible, and I was reduced to hearing six lectures a day — an experience which was at the time exacting, but which turned out to be singularly profitable. German books could wait to be read, but German masters could not be heard again. In that dreary winter, also, our first child was born and died, and left us sadly stricken. Yet this disciplinary period was in fact the beginning of lifelong association with German thought; the teaching to which I was soon called was, in the main, that of German theology and philosophy; and the books I wrote — if they had any value — were in large part applications of German learning. A half-dozen or more were translated into German; and the contact thus established was, I have always believed, one determining factor in promoting an adventure thirty years later, which in my student days would have seemed the most fantastic of dreams.

It was proposed in 1905 that an exchange of

professors should be arranged between the University of Berlin and Harvard University, and three names were transmitted by Harvard from which Berlin should select the first appointment. To my great astonishment I found myself designated to begin this novel undertaking of academic reciprocity. The appointment was probably made, in part, because my little books had become known in Germany to be innocuous, and in part also because the subjects with which I had become concerned were unfamiliar to German students. There were plenty of scholars at Harvard University of international reputation, but most of them were paralleled by ᴜen of equal distinction at Berlin. On the other hand, the problems of philanthropic and social reform, as they were being met in America, provided material which had at least the merit of novelty; and I had the privilege of lecturing during one semester at Berlin on 'Social Ethics in the United States.' It was an exhilarating interlude, which gave an opportunity to contrast the German system of governmental paternalism with the less organized but more flexible methods of private initiative in American philanthropy, and contributed, I hope, to the stabilizing of instruction in such subjects at Harvard University.

One incident in the course of this challenging venture was soon called to my attention, and tended to repress any inclination to complacency. It occurred to Professor Brandl, the well-known critic

ffriedrich August Gottreu Tholuck

of English literature, to advise his students that it might be to their advantage to attend my lectures, not because they cared to learn how the Americans administered their charities or organized their business, but because they would have an unusual opportunity to accustom their ears to the English language. As a result of this somewhat impersonal interest, it turned out that a considerable fraction of the students who registered, with apparent eagerness, as auditors, and remained most constant in their attendance, were listening, not to the teachings so sedulously adapted to German needs, but simply to the American accent and the New England twang.

Among the reminiscences of this return to German University life, the most enduring is that of stimulating companionship with the distinguished scholars who graciously accepted me as a colleague and guest. The happy surprise awaited me of finding these famous men, whose writings I had regarded with such veneration, so human and unassuming in their habit of life ; and the Waiting-Room (*Sprechzimmer*), which had seemed in Halle a mysterious cave from which Olympian demigods emerged to their lectures, prove to be in Berlin a place of genial fellowship, where one might sit with Paulsen as he munched his sandwich, or watch the fireworks of Harnack's inimitable talk. Harnack was not only, by common consent, the prince of lecturers, but in conversation a master of crackling aphorisms. When I commented, one day, with regret, on his adding to his multifarious duties the care of the new Royal Library, Harnack replied: 'Yes, my dear colleague, heaven, in this or any world, is in having one thing to do and time to do it; hell, here or hereafter, is in having four and twenty insignificant details (*Kleinigkeiten*) rending you asunder.' Again, when I asked his estimate of the English translation of one of his books, he gravely replied: 'It contained only three defects — ignorance of the German language, ignorance of the English language, and ignorance of the subject. In other respects, it was excellent' (*Sonst war alles recht gut*).

I must not dwell too frivolously on this academic interchange, which involved serious responsibility, and whose chief mission was to prepare the way for the succession of colleagues who were to follow. Some scepticism had been expressed, in the University circle at Berlin, concerning the advisability of welcoming an American invasion, but when it actually arrived it was received with genuine and generous hospitality, both from official dignitaries and from kindly colleagues; and the hope of fruitful results for both Universities seemed assured — a hope soon to be frustrated by the terrific calamity of war. It was a long road which thus led from the lecture-rooms of Halle in 1872 to those of Berlin in 1905; but as I look back on its unanticipated end and its unpromising beginning, I see that its start-

Friedrich August Gottreu Tholuck

ing-point was in the long, hard winter under the gracious guidance of the saintly Tholuck.[1]

FRIEDRICH AUGUST GOTTREU THOLUCK was born in 1799, at Breslau, the son of a handworker; and at the age of ten was taken from school and set to work at the bench to learn the art of a goldsmith. His

[1] The life and work of Tholuck are described in elaborate detail, with the piety of a disciple, by L. Witte (*Das Leben D. Tholuck*, 2 Bde. 1885, 1886, with a complete bibliography); in the addresses of friends at the celebration of his fiftieth year of academic service (*Dr. Tholuck's fünfzizjähriges Jubiläum, am. 2 December, 1870*); and in the eulogy by Professor Kähler after Tholuck's death (*August Tholuck, Ein Lebensabriss*, 1877).

The first of these bibliographical references revives a personal memory which may amuse those who are familiar with the dignified manner of German officials. Young Witte, the son of a professor long known in Halle through his precocious learning as '*Wunderkind Witte*,' accompanied as chaplain the distinguished Professor Dorner in a visit to America in 1874 to attend a Congress of the Evangelical Alliance. Having made the acquaintance of Dr. Witte in Halle, I went to welcome him in Boston, and on a certain Monday found him and his learned superiors at an obscure lodging known as Smith's Hotel, frequented for the most part by commercial travellers. On being presented to Professor Dorner, I inquired how he had passed the previous Sunday. He replied that they had asked for the nearest church and had been directed to the interesting building and ritual of King's Chapel. Returning to Smith's Hotel, they proposed to themselves to spend their Sunday afternoon, as they would in Germany, at some pleasant garden, where beer and music might offer them relaxation, and sought the advice of the manager of the hotel concerning such a resort. The only suggestion he could make for such a use of a Puritan Sabbath was to direct them to Chelsea Beach, then at the height of its repute for questionable entertainments and more than questionable characters. The black-coated scholars forthwith betook themselves to this gay resort, and reported to me that they had found the company, both of gentlemen and ladies, most hospitable, and the beer very good. What might have been the effect on their sacred mission to the Evangelical Alliance if an official of that organization had passed by on the other side and observed the scene is easier to imagine than to describe.

sight suffered from the flames employed in that trade, and his hands proved unskilful. One day in moulding a gold ring he melted the stone fast into the setting, and the indignant father concluded that the boy was not fit to be an artisan and might as well be degraded to the unremunerative life of a student. In later life the son was wont to exhibit this worthless ring as the symbol of his emancipation. The boy thus relegated to school proved to be an infant prodigy of intellectual acquisition. At the age of fifteen he had, it is said, some knowledge of not less than nineteen languages, including not only the prescribed studies of the school, Latin, Greek, and French, but an acquaintance with Arabic, Russian, Sanscrit, and Dutch. Discovering one day at a bookseller's a grammar without title, he identified it as a handbook of the Malay tongue, and added this new language to his list. Attaching himself at the same age to a professor of Arabic, he became an effective assistant, meantime keeping a diary in Latin or in French as his mood suggested.

A year later, he migrated to Berlin, with no means of self-support, and there, when eighteen years of age, became the favorite disciple of the distinguished Orientalist, Friedrich von Diez, who had been in the diplomatic service at Constantinople, and to whom Goethe had indited verses of affection. Through the influence of this devout and erudite man, whom young Tholuck called 'a worthy disciple of Jesus Christ,' the mind of the precocious youth was diverted from linguistic studies to religion, and he entered the University of Berlin in 1817, not, as he had anticipated, to study philology, but under the faculty of theology. Here he came under the influence of Schleiermacher, whom he later described as 'the Christian Socrates,' and of Neander, through whose commendation, though against the judgment of other examiners, Tholuck, when barely twenty-two years old, was appointed a *Privat-docent*, and proceeded to lecture on biblical antiquities.

Here began the prolific and diversified productiveness which was to continue for more than fifty years. In 1822 the University of Jena gave him a doctorate in philosophy for his study of Persian pantheism. In 1823 appeared his 'Doctrine of Sin and the Redeemer,' written to refute the teaching of the distinguished de Wette, in his didactic romance, 'Theodore, or the Religion of a Doubter,' and composed by Tholuck in what he called 'a stream of inspiration.' In 1825 he published his 'Illustrations of Oriental Mysticism,' which opened to great numbers of readers a new world of lyrical expression. In the same year he was designated Professor in the University at Halle, where he became at once a centre of devoted discipleship and an object of vigorous, not to say brutal, opposition.

Halle had become recognized as the stronghold of defiant rationalism, which the presence of a pietist or mystic incited to protest, and even to violence. Tholuck, on the other hand, had been in intimate relations with reactionary conservatives and with devout Moravians in Berlin, and was in fact transferred to Halle to neutralize or spiritualize its prevailing tone. His reception there was not reassuring. It was difficult for him even to obtain an adequate lecture-room, and his first lecture was greeted by disorder and abuse. He found, as he recorded, among the nine hundred students of theology in Halle, only the most insignificant and dull among his supporters, and over against these 'orthodox idiots' a formidable body of the more gifted and ambitious youth. His listeners waited for any pietistic word or phrase that might escape him, and greeted it with a violent rattling of the window curtains to symbolize their dissent. Certain colleagues went so far as to report evil of him to the Minister of Instruction, and the doors of many houses were closed against him. It was not until 1839 that he was reënforced by Julius Müller, and in 1843 the learned Hupfeld joined him as a representative of mediating theology. The first of these allies became famous for his elaborate study of the 'Christian Doctrine of Sin' and was distinguished by impertinent students from other teachers of the same familiar name as 'Müller the Sinner.' His erudite volumes are by this time for the most part forgotten, but his name has survived as that

Friedrich August Gottreu Tholuck

of the author of many incisive aphorisms, of which perhaps the most familiar is his dictum concerning the evolution of a Christian : 'A Christian,' said Müller, 'is never made, but always making. He then that is a Christian is no Christian.' Hupfeld, on the other hand, while a devout and well-read scholar, and known to his generation chiefly as a painstaking commentator on the Psalms. appears to have been somewhat lacking in evangelical fervor, and in a moment of playful irony was described by Tholuck to me as 'Hupfeld' — with a sniff — 'learned but dry' (*Gründlich, aber trocken*).

Thus began an academic career which continued for the extraordinary term of fifty-two years, marked by untiring and diversified productiveness, and represented by eleven volumes of collected works. In 1833 he was designated University Preacher, and for forty years his sermons were subjects both of warm approval and of unsparing censure. He was not, either as orator or prophet, one of the great preachers of Germany. His sermons, many of which were translated, bore the marks of being by-products of a student's life. They were brief and fervent homilies rather than contributions to the thought of the age ; often more ingenious than profound, artificial in form and sentimental in type. A vein of irony in his nature led him to fanciful treatments and alliterative divisions. '*Scheiden*' and '*Leiden*,' '*Anfang*' and '*Ausgang*,' '*Wegen*' and '*Segen*,'

79

Present-Day Saints

'*Geschieden*' and '*Geblieben*,' — catch-words of this nature marked the sections of his discourse. The note of appeal familiar in German preaching, 'Oh, my dear brethren!' 'Ah, my beloved hearers!' seemed to approach homiletical affectation rather than to express a scholar's message. To a listener from Scotland, bred in the tradition of Chalmers or Guthrie, or an Englishman who had listened to Liddon or Robertson, or an American who had read the sermons of Bushnell or followed the logic of Park or responded to the message of Channing, the preaching of Tholuck was likely to seem childlike in its simplicity and florid rather than restrained. It was not surprising that pietists heard him more willingly than scholars and that his congregations held more women than men. Yet the æsthetic effect of the University service under Tholuck's direction was searching and profound. The noble orchestral music which enriched worship, the resonant singing of grand and familiar chorals, and then the apparition in the high pulpit of the slight, ascetic figure, appealing with gentle sincerity and exuberant imagination to the emotions of religion or the consciousness of sin, offered a spiritual relief from the strain of academic study which many a student welcomed as a gift of the Lord's Day.[1]

[1] A translation of *Sermons on Various Occasions*, with notes by the translator, is appended to Professor E. A. Park's *Sketch of the Life and Character of Professor Tholuck*, 1840; and a special series of sermons on *Light from the Cross* was translated by R. C. L. Brown (3d edition, 1869). •

Friedrich August Gottreu Tholuck

If it must be admitted that Tholuck was not a preacher of the first rank, it is equally true that he was not one of the great theologians of Germany. The volume of his work is prodigious, and his diversified knowledge and amazing memory enriched his writings with allusions, antitheses, and comparisons, of striking and often illuminating originality. Yet the very diversity of his interests precluded the creation of any single work which could survive as his monument. What was written so swiftly, and with such immediate reference to the controversies of his own time, could not escape the fate of temporariness.

To this limitation must be added the fact that the habitual attitude of Tholuck's mind was defensive and apologetic rather than bold and creative. He found himself in the storm-centre of debate between the rationalists and reactionaries, and applied himself to the task of mediation and reinterpretation. He thus represented, in his own time, the desire now under other conditions again conspicuous, to bring into effective unity the results of modern criticism and the acceptance of ancient formularies — the decanting of old wine into new bottles. This task of a ' *Vermittler* ' was easily misconceived as involving indecision, and even insincerity, and was in fact not without risk of ambiguity or obscurantism. Tholuck was at heart a mystic, and it was the Oriental teaching of immediate communion with God which won his first intellectual passion. His 'Illustrations of Oriental Mysticism' was expressly designed, as he wrote in the Preface, to reprove those 'who are inclined to believe in no directing grace of God beyond the sphere of the Christian revelation.' In his academic position, however, he felt himself called to defend the prevailing orthodoxy, and encountered violent, and even abusive, opposition, both from those who suspected him to be a disguised reactionary and from those who believed him to be a timid radical. Neither group of extremists could understand, or even tolerate, his attempted harmony of 'undisguised theological criticism and spiritual sympathy with conventional pietism.'[1] The temper of debate in his time may be sufficiently illustrated by the indecent attack on him by the philologist Fritzsche, of Rostock, who did not restrain himself from speaking of Tholuck's teaching as 'the unscholarly zeal of a fanatic.'

This defensive attitude, however warmly it attached to him students who sought reassurance for their evangelical faith, and especially those who were preparing for the service of that faith in American seminaries, sets Tholuck quite apart from the epoch-making theologians of his time. Schleiermacher had boldly accepted the mystical experience as the foundation of Christian doctrine, and thereby had inaugurated a new era in German theology.

[1] Kähler. *August Tholuck. Ein Lebensabriss*, 1877, S. 39.

Friedrich August Gottreu Tholuck

Neander, the second formative influence of Tholuck's student life, had dedicated his comprehensive learn-to one colossal task, and his 'History of the Christian Church' remains a permanent memorial of his erudition and piety. Tholuck, on the other hand, could not detach himself from the temporary dissensions which beset him, and his writings, whether exegetical or homiletical, have, with few exceptions, had their day and ceased to be.

What was it, then, that gave this little man an almost unique position in his generation, and led the distinguished Richard Rothe, in 1854, to say: 'If I were called to name the man who in our time has had the widest and deepest influence on the Evangelical Church, I should unquestionably name Tholuck'? The answer to this question is beyond dispute. Tireless in production and animated in controversy as Tholuck was throughout his long career, he impressed himself chiefly by the singular purity and charm of his character and the daily habit of his kindly life. In a word, whatever limitations he had as a scholar, he was preëminent as a saint. It is not an accident that, among his voluminous contributions to theological literature, the book which has most completely met the test of time is his 'Hours of Christian Devotion,'[1] first issued in 1839 and reaching its eighth edition in 1870. This collection of addresses

---

[1] The English translation, by Robert Menzies, is from the seventh edition, with an Author's Preface by Tholuck.

and meditations, enriched by brief poetic passages, chiefly of his own composition, was designed, as Tholuck said, to 'give a view of the development, and an impartial and healthy portraiture, of the Gospel life of faith.' It was, he confesses, 'in place of being composed, rather an effusion.' 'I have spent,' he says, 'a whole lifetime in battling against infidelity with the weapons of apologetic science; but I have become ever more and more convinced that the way to the heart does not lie through the head, and that the only way to conversion of the head lies through a converted heart which already tastes the living fruit of the Gospel.' It is not surprising that this collection has had extraordinary acceptance in many languages as a precious handbook of devotion. Differences of creed are forgotten as one reads these lyrics of faith; diversities of administration do not disguise the one spirit.

At this point one meets the intimate relation which Tholuck maintained with individual students. His 'hours of Christian devotion' were in large part hours spent in private conversation or instruction, and it was here that he most impressed himself on other lives. Many an academic teacher, as he reviews his life, may be led, by reflecting on the career of Tholuck, to correct his own estimate of values. He remembers how often he was embarrassed by the invasion of personal interviews among the precious hours of his work. He had pledged his busy days to

Friedrich August Gottreu Tholuck

what seemed the central obligations of instruction and discipline, and they were interrupted and thwarted by fruitless conversations with unresponsive youths. It is not impossible, however, that as he looks back, years later, on the course of events, he may discover that what had seemed sheer waste of time and effort was in reality his most rewarding opportunity; and that many a student who has forgotten the teachings of the classroom remembers the kindly counsels or chastening admonitions of a sympathetic friend.

So, in a superlative degree, it was with the disciples of Tholuck. In the daily walks which were all the recreation he permitted himself, up and down the arbor of his garden when it rained or across the fields in fine weather, he might almost invariably be seen accompanied by a student on either side, and applying his Socratic skill to explore their docile minds. Here was where his playful irony felt itself most free. Nothing stimulated him more than a young sceptic. No one received such chastening rebuke as a conventional pietist. 'My young friend,' he said, on one of these leisurely excursions, 'what do you think about when you see this beauty of sky and earth?' and the youth, adapting himself to what he fancied the great man's mood, replied: 'Ah, Herr Geheimrat, I think of the wonderful bounty of our heavenly Father.' 'And what do you think about?' said Tholuck, turning to his other compan-

85

ion, who frankly and boyishly answered, 'Well, I don't know that I think of anything in particular.' 'My young friend,' said the saintly teacher, 'you have told the truth!'

Humor, it is true, in its finer forms, was not a conspicuous gift of Tholuck. There was nothing very subtle in his translation of my name into its German equivalent, and invariably greeting me as '*Herr Erbsen-Körper*' (Pea-Body). On the other hand, when, in his opinion, the sense of humor seemed lacking in his interlocutor, as in a Scotch student of my time, there was a cutting edge in Tholuck's sarcasm which was not so much pleasantry as reprobation. In this habitual and studied intimacy with youth Tholuck was, so far as I know, a unique figure of his time in the German universities. He held weekday meetings in his own home for conference and prayer. He made much of Christmas celebrations, gathering his students with German enthusiasm round the Tree. Young men from other countries, England, Scotland, and the United States, finding themselves in a strange environment, and stumbling among the obstacles of language and custom, felt themselves steadied and sustained by the parental care of the kindly old man, and the not less solicitous and gracious hospitality of his cultivated wife. Letters like the following, written on scraps of paper, were frequent arrivals in the modest lodgings of foreign students:

𝔉riedrich 𝔄ugust 𝔊ottreu 𝔗holuck

Dear Sir,

I celebrate my birthday, please God, with a few friends, sunday next evening. I am not sure if you or your dear lady will be able to participate, which would be most agreeable to both of us.

yours

A. Tholuck

Nor was this friendly concern limited to one's residence at Halle. Two years after my return, on receiving from America news of the birth of a child, Tholuck wrote as follows to its mother:

'MY DEAR FRIEND, — You have rejoiced both my wife and myself with the news of the new gift of God which has come to you, and I must add to my wife's letter some lines of my own. I send also to your husband our good wishes on his appointment as University Preacher. How happy should I be, now that I have withdrawn from that duty myself, to listen to him, and I fancy that something of the spirit of Schleiermacher may hover about him. For myself, I grow constantly weaker, and our theological attendance decreases. All the more therefore we turn to the rich resources of God. And so may God uphold us.

'Devotedly yours

'A. THOLUCK'

Present-Day Saints

Tholuck had made many journeys — not, as was once his intention, across the Atlantic — but to England, France, Spain, and Italy, where he was welcomed by the distinguished von Bunsen and served as chaplain in the German Evangelical Church. His table-talk was therefore curiously cosmopolitan under the conditions of so modest a home and so provincial a town. With his extraordinary command of languages, he would adapt his conversation to his companion, and indeed exhibit some satisfaction in using the niceties, or even the slang, of the foreign tongue. At times this philological accuracy did not conform to the common use of words. Thus, in speaking of his great preceptor, he surprised me one day by remarking, 'You know that Schleiermacher was a miscreant!' 'Dear me,' said I, 'I had always supposed him to be a very honorable character.' 'Ah, yes,' answered Tholuck, 'but in a physical sense he was a miscreant; what you call a humpback.' And indeed the portraits of the 'Christian Socrates' show him bowed down by the studious habits of his life.

The personal religion of each youth was to Tholuck of unending interest and inquiry. On learning, for example, that I had been bred in the Unitarian communion, he remarked, 'Ah, the Unitarians; they are mystics!' and in this passing comment revealed an insight into the spirit of representative Unitarians, like Martineau or Parker, or as expressed in the

Friedrich August Gottreu Tholuck

hymns of Longfellow or Hosmer, more observant than many nearer neighbors possessed. Readers of Theodore Parker, for example, have often failed to note in his 'Discourse of Matters Pertaining to Religion' the frank acceptance of the fundamental teaching of Schleiermacher, and even the adoption of the title used by that master for his first work.

Such, then, are some of the reminiscences which students of theology in Germany between 1850 and 1880 — now almost without exception departed this life — would desire to report of their days in Halle. They were responsive listeners to Tholuck's exegetical lectures and fervent discourses, wondering at the animation and vigor which could proceed from so frail and enfeebled a frame; but they brought back with them to their professorships and pastorates, as the ripest fruit of their German years, the assurance that the vocation of a scholar has room in it for humane and individualized beneficence. Other teachers may have seemed to them more profound, but none so illuminating and elevating. Tholuck's word, as was written of his Master, was made flesh and dwelt among us, and communicated by spiritual contagion its grace and truth.

CHAPTER V

EDWARD EVERETT HALE

THE second phase of a young minister's career is reached when he passes from his years of scholastic training to meet the practical problems of pastoral life. It is as a rule a chastening experience. The learning laboriously acquired seems to have little applicability to the needs of human souls; the sermons sedulously produced seem remote from reality; the conduct of free prayer proves to be an emotional excitation which tempts one to envy the adherents of prescribed and liturgical forms. The young aspirant finds himself stranded between the love of study and the cure of souls, and as he proceeds from church to church he recalls the unclean spirit which 'walketh through dry places, seeking rest, and finding none.' The very title of 'candidate' has about it a touch of self-seeking and mendicancy. It is true that in ancient Rome a candidate was clothed in a white toga to symbolize his guilelessness; but these applicants for office were tempted to become such obsequious place-hunters that they were described by Cicero as 'a much too civil breed'; (*officiosissima natio candidatorum*).

The most salutary way of escape from this experience is to cut loose from all familiar surroundings, drop from one's shoulders the white toga, and recover

Always y

E E Hale

Edward Everett Hale

self-confidence among strangers, who know nothing
of one's past and may even entertain the illusion of
one's competence. That was the rescue from self-
distrust which my father had found when he left
Cambridge and crossed the Alleghanies to a village
in western Pennsylvania; and a similar salvation by
migration was offered to me through the masterful
guidance of Edward Everett Hale.

Acquaintance with him was by no means a new
experience. During my college course he had been
at the height of his powers, and the great basilica
at the South End of Boston was thronged with
listeners. Mr. B. J. Lang, then the director of musical
taste in Boston, conducted a notable choir, and Dr.
Hale's message of coöperative citizenship boomed
across the church in his resonant voice to the back
pew into which I often slipped. In 1873 I had the
happiness of joining him during a part of his journey
in Europe, and watched the equal delight he had in
conferring with old Catholics in Munich and in collecting wild flowers in Switzerland. He was, as his
son and biographer has said, 'the best travelling
companion in the world,' observant, appreciative,
and playful.

When, however, in the autumn of 1873 I returned
from Germany and was confronted by the problem
of pastoral settlement, Dr. Hale's characteristically
romantic counsel was that I should abandon the
comfortable conditions of New England and find

myself by 'going West.' There happened to be at
that time a small college in Ohio, which had gained
some reputation under the direction of the distinguished educational reformer, Horace Mann. After
his death its declining fortunes had been reënforced by
contributions from Unitarians; but it still remained
a serious question whether the fame of Horace Mann
could overcome the deficit he had bequeathed.

Antioch College has of late become conspicuous
through the initiative and originality of a new administrator, whose programme and achievements Horace
Mann would have been the first to commend; but
in 1873 the college presented as forlorn and unexhilarating an environment as a youth fresh from a
German university, with his uncomplaining bride,
was ever called to enter. The region may have had
rural charm in summer, but in November it was
bleak and raw, and the roads were a sea of mud.
My wife and I were lodged in a rude dormitory, with
a huge air-tight stove filling the greater part of the
room, leaving just space for two rough cots in the
corners; and the choice had to be made between being
suffocated at night by over-heated iron or finding
our meagre pitchers of water crusted with ice in the
morning. The students were eager and responsive,
but quite distinguishable from the Harvard type.
On my first Sunday evening I had gathered a considerable group in the Common Room, and was
discoursing to them in the best manner of a Harvard

student. Suddenly, a rough voice interrupted me by shouting: 'I notice that you talk a lot about God. What do you mean by God? If you mean Force, why not say so?' It was a somewhat startling challenge, and it was not until after some weeks of acquaintance, and some long walks along the muddy roads, that I found this impetuous sceptic a temperamentally devout youth, who had been driven into materialism by the denunciatory creed offered to him as Christian truth.

Nothing could have been more disciplinary than this Spartan experience, of plain — indeed, very plain — living, and daily contact — indeed, daily contention — with unsophisticated, undisguised, and unconventional minds. The lessons there learned have long survived the lessons taught, and the friendships gained have outlived both. There was sagacity as well as romanticism in Dr. Hale's counsel that an overtrained and under-experienced student should precipitate himself into the deep waters of reality, where his spiritual life must swim or sink. If I were to offer general advice to young ministers — which would be as injudicious as it would be unheeded — I should deter them from undertaking conspicuous service for ten years or more, or from serving as assistants to older pastors, and should recommend professional isolation, an unfamiliar and even uncongenial environment, and the challenge of lives bred in ways remote from one's own.

Present-Day Saints

Returning from this wholesome though ascetic venture, and having rashly accepted the pastorate of the First Parish in Cambridge, I turned to Dr. Hale for his blessing, and he laid his hands on me in ordaining prayer, and continued throughout the few years of my parochial service as in a peculiar sense my father in God. Finally, on being designated to direct worship in the Chapel of Harvard University under a voluntary system, and with the coöperation of a Staff of Preachers, my first choice of a colleague and counsellor was Dr. Hale. He literally threw himself into the new project with joyous coöperation and fertile initiative. For three years he gave unstinted service to the University, devising plans of personal intimacy with students; concerning himself with the details of the Preachers' residential rooms; beginning there the collection of a Preachers' Library; hanging on the wall a portrait of George Washington, who had occupied the rooms as his headquarters until a cannon ball from the British lines intimated that the Craigie House, a half-mile away, was safer; and, in the casual manner which marked many of his most enduring works, noting on some loose pages the impressions made on him by his weeks of service, thus writing the first chapter of a precious and confidential book of records, in which successive preachers have narrated their achievements and disappointments, their hopes and fears. So for thirty-five years this rare and generous genius was associated with each step in my professional experience. Ordination for the ministry, received from his hands, had the character of indelibility which the Council of Florence in 1439 assigned to that rite.

Dr. Hale's career was so conspicuous in his generation, and his life and work have been described in such detail,[1] and are so affectionately commemorated in Lend-a-Hand societies and their multiplying offspring, that it might seem superfluous, if not presumptuous, to review them further. It has seemed, however, to some lovers of Dr. Hale that the very multiplicity of his gifts and activities may disguise from a later generation the peculiar quality of his character and influence. He still holds a place in literary history through the undiminished vitality of 'The Man Without a Country'; and 'In His Name'; he still remains the patron saint of many organizations founded on his famous maxims: 'Look up and not down; look out and not in; look forward and not back, and lend a hand'; his lifelike statue registers in bronze the gratitude of a city for his unstinted beneficence; yet none of these memorials seem to report with adequate emphasis the special characteristic which won the devoted loyalty and love of his disciples. It was the extraordinary lavishness of his affection, the prodigality of sympathy

[1] *The Life and Letters of Edward Everett Hale*, by Edward E. Hale, Jr., 2 vols., 1917.

with which he gave himself to the cause or the case which for the moment called to him. It was a virtue which involved at the same time a limitation, for this intense preoccupation with an immediate need might easily obstruct or delay a more serious obligation. His sermon for Sunday morning might have the marks of hasty preparation, but that might be because on Saturday a poor woman had sought his aid, and a home must be found for her at the cost of the whole precious evening. There was often this lack of perspective and proportion in his work ; the acceptance of more engagements than could be adequately filled ; the precipitate self-committal to a new idea or scheme without time or means to carry it through.

It happened, for example, that in one of our conversations he commended to me the writings of the mediæval mystics ; and during the forty years which have passed since that talk I have found elevating companionship in the literature to which I was thus led. Shortly after this initiation into that goodly fellowship I was astonished by receiving a long letter from Dr. Hale, written on scraps of paper torn from magazines, at a railroad junction where he had missed his connection. The letter itself has drifted away, but the purport of it was as follows :

'DEAR FRANK, —You and I, and one other person, to be later named, are to make a book similar to

Edward Everett Hale

Vaughan's 'Hours with the Mystics.' It will consist of a series of letters, written independently, and passed from one writer to the next. This is the first letter. You will comment on it and pass it to ——. When this correspondence has gone round three times there will be a book of nine chapters, and the subject we love will be given new life.

> 'Affectionately yours,
> 'EDWARD EVERETT HALE.'

Then followed a brief sketch of the mediæval mystics, interrupted, apparently, by the arrival of his train, and constituting, not only the first, but the last chapter ever produced of this precipitate but alluring enterprise.

This was the trait which delivered Dr. Hale into the hands of hostile critics, who found his historical erudition sometimes defective and his schemes often Utopian; but it was at the same time the quality which won, in an almost unique degree, a personal and affectionate devotion. The poor woman given lodging on Saturday night was not aware that the Sunday's sermon suffered, but she had learned what Jesus meant when he said, 'Inasmuch as ye have done it unto one of these my brethren, even these least, ye did it unto me.' The procession of mendicants, promoters, authors, and reformers which marched into his study found at last a man who believed in them, and who even endorsed their notes, at great

cost both of Dr. Hale's money and of criticism from
more prudent men. Young people with their dreams
and schemes found themselves, not objects of professional scrutiny, but sharers of a wealth of suggestion and enthusiasm; old people whose way had been
hard had their eyes opened and saw that this rough
road was leading them straight to the City of God.

This, rather than his literary gifts, became treas-
ured by young and old as:

> 'That best portion of a good man's life,
> His little, nameless, unremembered acts
> Of kindness and of love.'

An indomitable and contagious confidence in the
human soul; a discovery of the better self which
one's self had not yet found, and the application of
this better self to what Dr. Hale called 'The creation
of the possible Boston,' or 'The coming of the kingdom of God to our own doors'; the discovery
of dramatic interest in uninteresting lives, as though
it were written of him, as of his Master, that the
secrets of many hearts should be revealed — this
is the aspect of Dr. Hale's diversified and prodigiously
productive life which is cherished in the memory of
many grateful witnesses as the gift which assures
to him a permanent place among present-day saints.

EDWARD EVERETT HALE was born in 1822. His
father was the editor of an important organ of
Boston opinion, the 'Daily Advertiser,' and his

Edward Everett Hale

mother a sister of the eminent orator and statesman, Edward Everett. The instincts of journalism and literature were thus in his blood; and in his 'teens he contributed reviews and editorials to the 'Advertiser,' learned the art of shorthand reporting, and acquired the habit of rapid and confident composition. He entered Harvard College at what now appears the incredible age of thirteen and graduated in 1839, a member of the Phi Beta Kappa and Class Poet; though of this production he wrote at the time, 'It has convinced me, what I knew perfectly well before, that I am not nor ever could be a poet, or have the least claim to that title.' After various experiments in teaching, reporting, and writing, he committed himself to the profession of the ministry, not by attending a theological school, but by private reading under the direction of his pastor in Boston — an irregularity of procedure which he always, though with questionable arguments, insisted had been to his advantage in the profession.

His son and biographer has expressed the opinion that his father was 'not deeply impressed by the responsibilities and opportunities of the minister's life,' but was drawn to the profession as 'providing leisure for literary work.' It is difficult, however, to discover the signs of such half-heartedness in so whole-hearted and continuous a career. He began to preach at the preposterous age of twenty, and was called to the charge of an important church in

Worcester when but twenty-three. Literary leisure, if indeed he ever hoped for it, was never attained, but in the interstices of arduous pastoral duties his literary productiveness was resolutely maintained. Even in youth he was an impressive figure, tall and gaunt, with searching and appealing eyes, and with a voice so deep and resonant that it may be fitly described as a vocal organ. It was as though he pulled out one stop after another of his great instrument, until the very volume of sound might call to mind the lines of Dryden,

> 'Through all the compass of the notes it ran,
> The diapason closing full in man.'

His ministry, thus begun, assumed at once the twofold character which it maintained for sixty years. On the one hand, his conduct of worship was marked by unstudied simplicity. On the other hand, his religious ideal was applied to the social needs and problems of his community. Occasional essays in the 'North American Review' and the 'Boston Miscellany,' and articles in the 'Daily Advertiser,' satisfied his literary ambition and contributed to make his life in Worcester one of exhilaration and contentment. The preaching of a youth of twenty-three, however, could not express more than a healthy and joyous optimism. His social horizon was limited, and his literary work incidental. It was not until 1856, when, at the age of thirty-four, he was called to a church in Boston, that his maturing powers

Edward Everett Hale

expressed themselves, his social service became comprehensive, and his writings a permanent contribution to American literature. 'Steeped in literature from his birth,' says his son, 'and coming to maturity very early, he produced nothing of artistic quality until he was thirty-seven years old.' Indeed, on undertaking the larger work in Boston, he made definite resolutions to restrain his divergent tastes, or, in his own words : 'First, to give more care to my work and write sermons of permanent value ; second, to cut loose from "The Examiner" and other avocations ; third, to devote myself exclusively to my parish and refuse all other duties.'

It soon proved quite impossible, however, to hold his imagination and vitality within such bounds, and his social service was soon enlarged by the establishment of a mission chapel, and by the promotion of a districting-plan of poor-relief, under the system proposed by Chalmers, and organized in Boston as The Benevolent Fraternity of Churches.

Hardly had these extraneous activities defeated his good resolution of concentration than the war of 1861 broke on the unprepared North, and the scheme of a limited and pastoral service was completely submerged by the tide of patriotism. Drilling of young soldiers, and promoting of further enlistments, alternated with sermons on the crisis. 'On Sunday,' he writes, 'I shall preach on "Taking the Loan," from John VI. 12, or Matthew V. 42.' The first passage was perhaps applied to the small givers: 'Gather up the fragments that remain, that nothing be lost'; while the second was more calculated to reach the prudent rich, 'From him that would borrow of thee turn not thou away.' Thus the war, as has often happened under the strain of a great crisis, discovered Edward Everett Hale to himself; and he became, not only a preacher, or what is called a social worker, but a national figure, inspiring and exhorting by word and pen. 'Until 1861,' he said of himself, 'I was only known in Boston as an energetic minister of an active church; then the war came along and brought me into public life, and I have never got back into simple parish life again.'

The most permanent memorial of this passionate patriotism was his hastily written, but irresistibly appealing, story, 'The Man Without a Country.' Fiction provided for him the most convincing form of argument, and he applied himself to make, as he later wrote, 'a contribution, however humble, toward the formation of a just and true national sentiment, a sentiment of love to the nation.' Published anonymously, and professing to be written by an officer of the Navy, the tale had at once a prodigious effect. By many readers its impossible situations were believed to be historical, and it was pointed out by some critics that the facts of Philip Nolan's life had not been accurately stated. In a word, the preacher had been led, in the passion of a national emergency, to discover where his homiletical aims might have their widest channel of utterance. Others might preach in sermons or poems, while he could preach best in story-telling. Others could urge enlistments, subscribe to loans, or fight for the Union, while he could show the tragic fate of a man without a country.

In one of the delightful 'Letters' of Maurice Hewlett he offers the same defence of the story-teller. 'They say it is romance,' he wrote of one of his novels, 'I say it is history. I am sure my notion of giving real history this form, of illuminating history from within, is a sound one.' That was precisely the contribution of Dr. Hale to patriotism. He illuminated history from within; and his tale, which on examination is obviously fictitious, has preached patriotism to three generations of American youth, and still provides good material for moving-picture shows. There is an interesting analogy here with the achievement of Julia Ward Howe in her 'Battle Hymn of the Republic.' That stirring lyric, as she herself reports, was conceived during a restless night and written out the next morning; yet it not only met the needs of a critical hour but has lifted loyalty into sacred song for generations then unborn. Few parallels could be found with the vitality for over sixty years of Mrs. Howe's verses and of Dr. Hale's story. Critics may still insist that he was not a historian but a romanticist; but he would himself be well contented if it could be said of him, in Hewlett's words, that he illuminated history from within.

From this point of self-discovery Dr. Hale was led on to apply his art of preaching through fiction in the most varied forms of suggestion and disguise. He had already let loose his imagination with playful exaggeration in 'My Double, and How He Undid Me' (1856), 'a wholly impossible conception,' his biographer says, 'dealt with in an absolutely matter-of-fact way,' but in its effect a plea for mercy to over-worked parsons. There soon followed a continuous stream of Utopian romances, historical memorials, biographical studies, and sketches of a Christianized social order, which became simply overwhelming in its volume and velocity. His collected 'Works,' in ten volumes, comprise only a fragment of the amazing total. No complete bibliography of his writings is known to exist; but a publishers' list of early productions, from 1848 to 1894, contains the titles of eighty-two volumes, issued in forty-six years, and Dr. Hale himself confesses to 'fifteen or sixteen hundred sermons.' When, however, one reviews these diversified publications, whether candidly serious or exuberantly imaginative, they are seen to be, not evidences of divisive interests, but essentially the manifold expressions of a single aim. With all their variety of treatment, they are in intention nothing but sermons. Fiction, history, economics, and poetry, are all utilized to illustrate what might happen, as the title of one essay asks, 'If Jesus came to Boston?' Some critics have censured Dr. Hale for dissipating powers which might have had more permanent effect if applied to any one of his various schemes. The fact is that what seems undiscriminating and precipitate is but the overflow of preaching power, the by-products of a profession which took all life for its province. 'Sybaris and Other Homes' is a fanciful disguise for a treatise on social hygiene. 'How They Lived at Hampton' reveals its didactic purpose in the sub-title, 'A Story of Practical Christianity Applied to the Manufacture of Woolens.'

This essentially homiletical intention is sufficiently indicated when one recalls the two writings of Dr. Hale which would be generally regarded as having, together with 'The Man Without a Country,' a permanent place in literary history. The first is his 'Ten Times One is Ten,' which was issued as a serial in his magazine 'Old and New,' in 1870, but which soon became the inspiration of scores of organizations and of thousands of lives. It begins, as everybody knows, and as all of Dr. Hale's Utopias begin, with the most elementary situations. Ten friends of Harry Wadsworth resolve to live as he would have them, to look up and not down, to look forward and not back, to look out and not in, and to lend a hand. Each of them proposes, still further, to get ten other enlistments in the same faith. Then the amazing mathematical process takes place, which less praiseworthy enterprises have applied, in more questionable forms, to chain-letters or cumulative mendicancy. Within a term, reckoned at about twenty-seven years, the entire population of the world finds itself enrolled in Harry Wadsworth Clubs, and the Kingdom of God has taken possession of the globe. The fascinating dream seized on the imagination of readers, and there were soon evolved, not only Lend-a-Hand Clubs, but Look-Up Legions, King's Daughters, and many other far-reaching organizations, which either directly appropriated the mottoes or applied the same method of growth. The fertilizing effect of the story-teller's art had made the parish minister in Boston a missionary to uncounted millions of souls.

The second, and in its form and treatment the most painstaking and ambitious of Dr. Hale's writings, was 'In His Name.' 'My father,' says his son, 'generally thought of "In His Name" as his best book.' Here again the homiletical *motif* is as obvious as in 'Ten Times One is Ten.' A Christmas story — for that was its original form — should describe discipleship in terms of simple loyalty and courage. In this case, however, the writer believed that the scene would appear more dramatic if it were detached from modern life, and he uses the touching history of the early Waldensians as his stage. He visited the region where ever since the twelfth century they had maintained their simple faith; he reviewed the story of the merciless persecutions which they endured; he tramped over the hills which look down on Lyons; and there are few passages in modern literature more vivid and geographically accurate than the detailed account of the fearless riders on their errand of mercy to the sick child. It has seemed to some critics that this touching and dramatic narrative became somewhat overladen with these local and historical allusions, and that its course was interrupted by the prolonged interlude of the troubadour's song and the legend of Aucassin and Nicolette. Dr. Hale could not touch any theme lightly, but must throw himself into each detail and explore each circumstance; and it may be not unreasonable to maintain that the picturesqueness of mediævalism tempted the author to needlessly laborious research. On the other hand, he must be a hardened critic who can read of this secret fellowship, with its imperative watchwords and its unquestioning obedience, without real emotion, and it is not surprising that many a modern organization of discipleship has found a sufficient creed in the maxims: 'For the love of Christ,' and 'In His Name.' Indeed, the evidence that this elaborate tale is in effect a sermon for the modern world is expressly given in its last chapter: 'It is always going on, Philip. Jesus Christ is giving life more abundantly, and awakening the dead now, just as he said he would. . . . Five hundred years hence, dear Phil, they will publish a story about you and me. We shall seem very romantic then ; and we shall be worth reading about, if what we do is simple enough, and brave enough, and loving enough for anybody to think we do it "for the love of Christ," or for anybody to guess that we had been bound together "In His Name."'

These instances are sufficient to indicate the range and versatility of Dr. Hale's literary gifts. Meantime, what was the effect of these varied excursions into fiction and history on the special vocation of the preacher, of which they were the delightful by-products? Sermons and the conduct of worship remained his duty and delight until the end of his life. Even after his retirement from the pastorate, he accepted service as Chaplain of the Senate at Washington, and his 'Prayers in the Senate in 1904' remains as an appealing testimony to his undiminished hope and faith. On June 6, 1909, which happened to be Whitsunday, he was eighty-seven years old ; and wrote : 'Dr. Temple has forbidden me to preach to-day — the first Whitsunday in sixty-five years without a Whitsunday sermon.' Four days later, on June 10, he died.

From about the year 1880 he had permitted many of his sermons to be printed, and hundreds of them had been circulated as tracts or collected in volumes. The form of these sermons, however, becomes more

Edward Everett Hale

unstudied as the years pass, and a few great themes, in their infinitely varied ways of expression, become his reiterated and dominant message. In his earlier period no problem of civic, national, or theological interest escaped his alert observation, and such subjects as 'The Abolition of Pauperism,' 'Sunday Laws,' 'The Possible Boston,' 'The Centenary of the Constitution,' occur among his discourses. It should not be said that his later preaching was less comprehensive or humane; but it becomes evident that the dream of coöperative consecration reported in 'Ten Times One is Ten,' and the sufficiency of a life lived 'In His Name,' called to him on almost every Sunday for amplification and varied application. A clever woman who had listened to various preachers at Harvard University remarked that each of them used a certain word which recurred like a *motif* in his conduct of worship. Dr. Brooks's word, she said, was *Richness* — the unrealized wealth of human opportunity and blessing; Dr. Hale's word was *Together* — the cumulative force of associated discipleship. Whenever the community or the University needed a reënforcement of spiritual power Dr. Hale's message was 'Together.' Thus he became more and more the voice of the city's conscience and the unofficial chaplain of each municipal event or national crisis.

The climax of this spiritual authority was reached when, largely through his initiative, a mass meeting was held on the night of December 31, 1900, to mark the transition to a new century. A vast throng packed the space from the State House in Boston nearly to Tremont Street and waited in solemn stillness for the coming of midnight. A few moments before the hour struck Dr. Hale's words, transmitted by a sounding board, swept across the darkness, as if a messenger from the skies were speaking : 'Lord, Thou hast been our dwelling-place in all generations!' Then, as the distant bells struck the hour, trumpets blew, and the great concourse joined with Dr. Hale in repeating the Lord's Prayer and in singing 'America.' It was a scene which no one could witness without emotion, or can recall without hearing again the far-reaching voice of the unseen preacher. The multitude had gathered like the companions of 'Ten Times One is Ten,' and welcomed a new century 'In His Name.'

Such, in brief, were the nature and effect of Dr. Hale's later ministry — an increasing simplicity in teaching, and a spiritual authority attained by many years of self-effacing service. His talks to students at Harvard University had the directness of an old man's confidential conversation. More and more his thought and desire turned to individuals, and the estimate which he made of his service was based on his approach, not to great audiences, but to single lives. Thus, in the 'Book of Records' maintained by the Preachers to the University he writes: 'I met on May 4th some twenty undergraduates of all classes, to talk on the choice of a profession, and conversed with them for two hours.' And again : 'I find that I have memoranda of calls from sixteen students. . . . I said something about prayer one morning in a sermon which sent into this room the next Saturday a man who had not heard the sermon, and I fancy had not heard ten sermons in his life. He told me his father was an agnostic, and didn't wish his children to attend any church. But this man was passionately anxious that I might show him how he might with a good conscience pray to the "Power which makes for righteousness." He would never have come near me but for a sermon which he did not hear, but which had been talked about at his boarding-house.'

There has been at times an inclination, both among meticulous scholars and among intolerant reformers, to regard Dr. Hale as lacking in persistency, either of thought or of action. He would fling himself, it has been said, into a historical problem, like that of the Waldensian maxims, and soon be diverted to take part in a municipal campaign or a crusade for peace. One who could so plausibly make fiction look like history might be easily tempted to embellish history with fiction. A playful cynic, observing these multitudinous avocations, once called him 'Edward Everything Hale,' and it must be admitted that this extraordinary diversity of interest did preclude the possibility of continuous leadership in any one direction. Dr. Hale's gift was for inspiration, rather than for organization; it was for him to initiate, rather than to demonstrate. Yet this facile shifting of enthusiasm, and this passion for originality, were precisely the qualities which endeared him to his disciples, and especially to young people with their unrealized and often visionary hopes. A young man would bring his scheme or dream to Dr. Hale and, as the old man reinterpreted it, it seemed to grow more practicable and sane than the schemer or dreamer had imagined. 'Here at last,' the youth would say, 'is one who understands me; now I can trust my dream and be obedient to my vision.'

It is reported that in a conversation between Herbert Spencer and Thomas Huxley, the philosopher said, 'I suppose that all one can do with his life is to make his mark and go!' to which, with greater wisdom as well as modesty, the biologist replied, 'Ah, that is too much to expect. All that one can do is to give a push!' That is almost precisely what Dr. Hale did for many lives. He did not always leave his mark on them, and they might follow paths and reach ends which he had not suggested, and might not even have approved; but he had given them the push they needed, the momentum of the spirit, the propulsion of a new idea. He was a sower, rather than a harvester or sifter. As he sowed, some seed fell by the wayside, and the hungry critics devoured it; some

Edward Everett Hale

fell on hard subjects, where it could not take root; some among thorns of controversy, where it was choked by newly discovered facts; but here and there the seed, so prodigally scattered, fell in congenial soil, and brought forth a harvest of which more cautious scholars could not dream. The most abiding quality of this gifted, versatile, and generous friend was the complete dedication of a long life to thoughts and deeds of self-effacing service. The text which came to be most reiterated by him, and which was most suggestive of him during his last years, was the majestic summons: 'I am come that they might have life, and that they might have it more abundantly.' That was his test of theology, politics, philanthropy, books, people. Did they generate or disseminate a more abundant life? It is as life-giver and life-saver that he is to be given his place in the goodly fellowship of present-day saints.

CHAPTER VI

CHARLES CARROLL EVERETT

SIX short years were all that I was permitted to enjoy of a parish ministry, and even these were repeatedly interrupted by persistent illness; so that I spent nearly as many months in health-hunting in the East and West as in the doing of pastoral duties. My father had died of tuberculosis when only forty-nine, and many of my devoted parishioners anticipated my own early demise. If any good can be traced to this term of fragmentary service, it must be assigned, I have always believed, to the generous thoughts and prayers of the congregation for their minister during his absence, rather than to his unripe and intermittent deliverances from the pulpit.

On reviewing this brief and thwarted ministry, I derive from it one lesson which may be of interest to young parsons. The breaking-point among the varied duties of a first settlement is likely to be found, not in what is called parish work, or even in the composition of sermons, but in the strain imposed, under the method of non-liturgical churches, by the conduct of free prayer. A young man with eager desire to interpret the needs of his congregation finds himself summoned to moods of feeling and evidences of faith which are probably not yet within

C. C. Everett

his own experience, and which he must anticipate in order to express. The whole area of domestic trial and sorrow must be entered by him with the consolation of bereavement and the communication of hope. To a susceptible youth the emotional excitation thus involved is extreme, and many a young minister has realized with surprise that the chief strain, physical as well as spiritual, in the conduct of worship, is not, as he had anticipated, in the delivery of his sermon, but in the vicarious sharing of the experiences of his congregation through the offering of prayer in their behalf.

A beginner in the pastorate of a free church should, therefore, take very seriously his preparation for public prayer. He should acquaint himself with the noble collects of the early Church and use them in the formal introduction or conclusion of worship; he should compose in writing the outline of his own thought, to gain precision and continuity in his prayer, and to adapt his words to the special needs of trial or blessing which the approaching Sunday should recognize. On the other hand, he should guard as the highest privilege of his vocation the opportunity of freedom in prayer, and the applicability of prayer to immediate and personal needs or hopes. Fixed and traditional petitions afford the dignity, spaciousness, and familiarity which give them their place both in the approach to worship and in the expression of universal desires; but they are likely to miss the note of personal need, or of special incidents of sorrow or joy. It happened at a funeral service in my own family circle that the officiating priest was so addicted to the impersonal use of his printed text that he committed to God the 'soul of our brother here departed' when it was in reality a mother's body which lay before her mourning children.

Least of all should the different habits of mind and form of speech involved be disregarded or combined. Fixity of ritual contributes to distinction of phrase, reverent association with the past, and the sense of 'common prayer.' Freedom in prayer permits variation, applicability, fervor, and simplicity. Each has its place in worship; the one representing the congregation as an organic part of the universal Church, the other the single soul with its intimate desires, thanksgivings, and penitence. The free churchman has the happy privilege of utilizing both the treasures of the past and the needs of the present. He prays as one 'who shall be judged by the law of liberty.' The same poet who has most brilliantly satirized :

> 'That droning vacuum of compulsory prayer
> Still pumping phrases for the Ineffable,
> Though every valve of memory gasp and wheeze,'

has also confessed the incomparable experience of

> 'That perfect disenthralment which is God,'

Charles Carroll Everett

and that

'Power more near my life than life itself,
·   ·   ·   ·   ,   ·   ·
Missed in the commonplace of miracle.'

In 1880, after a second prolonged absence from pastoral service, it became evident that a parish ministry must be abandoned, and I was, as it then seemed, demoted to temporary duty in the Harvard Divinity School, where I might perhaps communicate to youths just arming themselves for the ministry the lessons of my own defeat. What seemed a calamity turned out, as often happens, to be an opportunity, for I found myself at once concerned with a transition in professional education which was unprecedented and challenging, and which opened the way to forty years of academic life.

Few intellectual satisfactions are more substantial and permanent than that which is found in doing, or in having a slight part in doing, something really new. I have had the rare privilege, during the experience of academic service, of being associated with not less than three such ventures of faith; each of which was met by much scepticism or opposition, but all of which, through the persistent devotion of a few confident advocates, have become institutionalized, or even venerable. One of these academic revolutions was that which transformed a denominational seminary into an undenominational school of theology, strictly analogous with the other professional schools of a university, and demanding as the first qualification in its teachers, not sectarian zeal, but adequate learning and religious catholicity. Another such venture was in the introduction of studies in modern social problems, as appropriate, not only for professional experts, but for young men about to enter the varied careers of the modern world. Still another step into the unknown was taken when the conduct of worship in Harvard University was freed from compulsion, and offered as a privilege to young men, under a plan of unconstrained and unsectarian religion — a plan which forty years ago was regarded with much apprehension, but which has now become not only thoroughly established but repeatedly imitated.

All of these momentous undertakings had behind them the propulsive force of President Eliot's decisions, and were regarded by him as among the most significant achievements of his administration ; but each of them was guided or sustained by an intermediate personality, whose wisdom and faith were essential factors in the transition. The first was directed by a secluded scholar ; the second was sustained by a man of business ; the third was reinforced by the greatest of modern preachers, whose academic service was but a by-product of his career. It is difficult to refrain from allusion to many other scholars and saints who have adorned Harvard University

118

during the last forty years, and with many of whom I have had the privilege of intimacy in their domestic experiences of sorrow or joy. Indeed, one is tempted in old age to idealize the past, and to see in that earlier generation, with all its limitations as teachers, a quality of urbane and gracious humanism which is not easy to maintain under the highly specialized and departmental conditions of an expanding university. I refrain, however, from extended enumeration, and recall in this and the two following chapters only those friendships which are associated with unprecedented incidents in academic history, and which reveal the personal sources of notable events.

The first of these academic transitions occurred in 1880 and the following years, in the Divinity School of the University. This professional seminary had existed for more than fifty years when President Eliot's administration began, and had for the whole of that period represented the Unitarian branch of Congregationalism. The endowment of the school had been almost entirely contributed by Unitarians, and it had become practically a training school for the ministers of Unitarian churches. The seven presidents of Harvard University, from President Kirkland, who was inaugurated in 1810, to President Hill, who resigned in 1868, were all members of that communion, and five of them were or had been Unitarian ministers. The faculty of the school during that period was distinguished by the names of

Present-Day Saints

Andrews Norton, Henry Ware, father and son; John Gorham Palfrey, George R. Noyes, and Convers Francis, all representing the same theological position, and its active apologists.

The alert and comprehensive foresight of President Eliot soon recognized that such a denominational seminary was not an appropriate department of a great university; and he believed, moreover, as a loyal Unitarian, that the principles of his own faith made an expansion of the school, not a surrender, but a testimony to its ideal of Christian unity. His confidence in this interpretation of the Unitarian tradition was reënforced by a phrase which the founders of the school, themselves Unitarians, had used, and which, I suppose, is unique among the constitutions of theological seminaries. It announced that 'Every encouragement shall be given to the serious, impartial, and unbiased investigation of Christian truth, and that no assent to the peculiarities of any denomination of Christians be required either of the instructors or students.' This fundamental clause had, in fact, deterred from sympathy the very persons it was designed to conciliate; for few students, or even professors, of theology had conceived of a divinity school as anything but an agent in propagating a sectarian creed, to which teachers should be pledged and in which students should be indoctrinated. Theology as a science, correlated with law or medicine,

120

with the same method of free research and the same spirit of singleminded devotion to truth, had practically no recognition among American seminaries; and a school in which 'no assent to the peculiarities of any denomination of Christians shall be required of professors or students,' was a spiritual enterprise which lay quite beyond the bounds of denominational zeal. The Harvard Divinity School was thus committed to the scientific method in the study of theology. To Unitarians who were primarily concerned with the promotion of a sect such action looked like the surrender of a strategic position; but it was in fact a convincing expression of the higher Unitarianism, which could welcome without apprehension the intercommunion of creeds, and was prepared to submit its own faith to the test of comparison. It was a withdrawal from Unitarian propagandism, but a triumph of Unitarian magnanimity.

In conformity with this idea, the curriculum of the school was promptly modernized, by the transfer of Hebrew to an elective study, and by the provision for intruction in the principles of philanthropy and social service. The faculty of the school was enlarged by the addition of two scholars of the Baptist communion and two of the Orthodox Congregational communion, and it was not many years before the students represented eight Protestant denominations. These and many other modifications created a completely new environment for theological studies, and aligned them so definitely with other departments of the University that courses in the Divinity School were accepted for non-theological degrees, and were in many instances attended by more students under other faculties than under that of theology. Finally, a coöperative relation was established with three other theological schools, and the dream cherished by James Freeman Clarke of a theological university was in some degree realized.

This unprecedented, and as it seemed to many, Utopian plan of President Eliot, depended, however, for its fulfilment on securing a sympathetic and sagacious agent within the school itself; and there were few characteristics of President Eliot's administration more striking than his gift of discovering in each case the right man to do the work, and then trusting him to do it. The revolution in the teaching of the law, the expansion and unification of the Faculty of Arts and Sciences, and many other academic achievements of the last fifty years, were due, not only to the initiative of the President, but to the sagacity and singlemindedness of his representatives. Such selective discrimination was peculiarly necessary in the case of the Divinity School; for its administrator must not only welcome new methods, but maintain unimpaired a sacred tradition of spiritual power and genuine piety. The Dean of the School must be not only recognized as a scholar but revered as a saint.

Charles Carroll Everett

Fortunately for the Harvard School, the man was at hand; and when, in 1880, I enlisted in its service, the new dean had just completed his first year in that office. For twenty-two years more he continued to adorn the school both by his learning and his character, and to environ the little group of students for the ministry with a serene and transparent atmosphere of Christian saintliness. The unknown author of the 'Theologia Germanica' wrote that he 'would fain be to the Eternal Goodness what a man's hand is to a man.' There was the same sense of attachment felt by all the faculty of that time toward its dean. We were well contented if we could reënforce his purposes as a man's hand serves a man. To me, as the youngest of the staff, he was both father-confessor and delightful companion. I lived round the corner from his home, and when problems of duty or instruction were difficult, I could climb the fence between and consult his parental wisdom. For many years we trudged together through the dark to the service of worship conducted by students on Friday evenings, arriving at the thinly attended gathering in time, as the dean would playfully say, 'to avoid the rush,' and sharing the experience — sometimes uninspiring, but sometimes most appealing — of listening to the first sermons perpetrated by our pupils, and discerning, if we might, the often obscure indications of ripening powers.

Nothing disturbed the serenity of the dean's faith

in the larger mission of the school. 'How interesting it is,' he remarked one night, 'to be concerned with something which only a few dozen persons in the world believe in!' It was said of Emerson that he took down the ancient idols from their niches so gently that it seemed an act of reverence. With the same gentleness of demeanor — and there was much of Emerson in his character — Dr. Everett met the reproaches of protesting denominationalists, and directed a work of academic iconoclasm so that it looked like an act of reverence. It was an inestimable privilege to a young man, trained only as a parish minister and conscious of insufficiency for the academic life, to be thus in daily intimacy with a revolutionist who was a conservative, and a theologian who was a saint.

CHARLES CARROLL EVERETT was born in Brunswick, Maine, in 1829, the son of a much respected lawyer of that college town. He was a youth of delicate constitution, and early lost the use of one eye, so that his range of reading was always restricted and, as has often happened under such limitations, was almost wholly devoted to the best literature. He was never closely informed about current events, but extraordinarily at home among the great poets and the masters of style. Hours that most persons waste in discursive reading were applied by him to reflection, and his thinking became singularly original and unprompted. His physical frailty became in later years, when his learning was beyond question, an amusingly effective weapon of argument. Thus, when it was proposed in the Harvard faculty to require an applicant for scholarship aid to pass a physical examination, and give reasonable promise of living long enough to justify the investment, Dean Everett gently intimated that such a condition would have ruled him quite out of consideration, and that his own parents were in doubt whether he was 'worth raising'; whereupon the motion to apply a physical test of scholarly promise was promptly withdrawn.

The youth graduated from Bowdoin College in 1850, and, either by his father's wish or his own inclination to observe and analyze, applied himself at first to the study of medicine. Philosophical reflection soon became, however, a dominating mood, and the care of the body less appealing than the study of the mind. He thereupon departed for two years of study in German universities, where he met the full efflorescence of Hegelian thought, of which he was to become a convinced and erudite expositor. 'First in the lectures of Professor Gabler,' Everett later wrote, 'and afterwards in the works of Hegel himself, I found the rudiments of a system of logic that charmed me with its beauty and simplicity.' For most students, it may be remarked, even if beauty may be discovered in the Hegelian logic, simplicity is not the word which comes first to mind. Young Everett was called back from Germany to Bowdoin College as instructor in modern languages, and it was proposed to advance him to a professorship. His theological views had, however, become difficult to adjust to the tests of orthodoxy prescribed by benefactors of the College, and his appointment was refused by its overseers. The not unnatural consequence of this rejection was to confirm the tendencies which were officially deplored, and Everett turned to the ministry of liberal religion as his vocation, and entered the Harvard Divinity School, graduated in 1859, and was at once called to his only pastoral charge, in Bangor, Maine.

In this isolated but congenial service, which continued for ten happy years, he found time to set his German studies in literary form and to complete the remarkable book on 'The Science of Thought' which for the first time expounded Hegelian logic to American readers in language which gave it, as Everett had hoped, 'beauty and simplicity.' To many minds, indeed, this was the first book which made thinking in itself reasonable; for the scholastic learning it contained was clothed in language of charm and wit, such as later captivated readers in the writings of William James. The headings of sections are abstract, formal, and even repellent; but the treatment is vivacious, concrete, and entertaining. The 'Logic of Language,' for example, leads to

Charles Carroll Everett

a lively discussion of idioms and slang in various
countries; and a chapter so unpromising as that on
'Static Induction' begins, 'If I put my hand into a
bag of marbles.' What other book discussing 'Cate-
gories of Thought' and 'Mediated Propositions'
ever had as its first words a dedication to the author's
wife, as perfect in form and spirit as the succeeding
pages are searching and profound?

> 'A garland fresh with flowers of song
>   Would be an offering more meet
> For thine acceptance than these sheaves
>   Of ripened, dry, and heavy wheat,
> Which, bringing from the harvest field,
>   I lay, beloved, at thy feet.
>
> 'I will not try with useless words
>   To glorify this gift of mine.
> It were a hopeless task to prove
>   The homely offering fit or fine.
> The truth is simply told: these sheaves
>   Are all I have; I make them thine.
>
> 'But when I sought the harvest field,
>   Thy careful love went forth with me,
> Supplied the strength I lacked, and wrought,
>   Through the long hours, ungrudgingly;
> Even this poor gift I cannot give;
>   I bring but what belongs to thee.'

Meantime, the secluded scholar had become a
beloved pastor and a conspicuous citizen, representing both city and state on public occasions; and the
affection of his parishioners may be inferred from
the comment of one of them to whom I ventured to

say, 'At any rate, you cannot call Dr. Everett handsome!' to which the loyal lady replied, 'Down at Bangor we think one eye becoming.'

The book and the pastorate soon had their natural consequence. In 1869, Dr. Everett was called to a professorship in the Harvard Divinity School, and his coming was like a fresh breeze from Northern Maine, reviving and invigorating academic life. He brought with him the two qualifications for instruction which young candidates for the ministry needed to assimilate — a rich pastoral experience and a consistent science of thought. The most immediate impression was made by his intimate and vivacious talks on the practical problems of a minister's life; and his flashes of wit and satire have become maxims and warnings to a whole generation of preachers. 'Lend your influence,' he would say, 'to any worthy cause of public need, but be careful not to lend your influence until you have it.' 'Let the music run through the service, but not run away with the service.' 'Prayer is not preaching, or a defining of one's position.' 'Do not "make" a prayer. Enter into the mood where prayer makes itself.' 'To regard baptism as a worthless rite because the child does not understand it is as if we postponed the mother's kiss for the same reason.' 'Ministerial intercourse is not the bread of life. Isolation means independence. The Penobscot Conference met every time I went into my study.'

Charles Carroll Everett

Much more serious in intention, and remaining as the permanent monument of Dr. Everett's career, were his two courses of lectures on Theology, which for thirty years made the substance of his work. The first, an introductory section, had the general title, 'The Psychological Elements of Religious Faith.' The second, and more extended series, covered the whole area of Christian doctrine under the title, 'Theism and the Christian Faith.' Both of these elaborate and extended discussions were given without manuscript and with a scrap of crumpled paper as the speaker's only guide; and when after his death it seemed a duty to publish his teachings they had to be gathered, by the scrupulous care of a devoted young colleague, from the notebooks of students; and it was a task of painstaking editorship to convey a just impression of the master's thought. From step to step the author proceeds, from religion as feeling, through the sense of the supernatural, to the final definition of religion as 'a feeling toward a supernatural presence manifesting itself in truth, goodness, and beauty.' The second course begins where the first one ends; and proceeds from the Unknowable of Spencer, through the various arguments for theism, to the exposition of 'Christianity as the absolute religion,' enlarging the definition of religion by adding 'as illustrated in the life and teaching of Jesus, and as expressed in every soul that is open to its influence.'

129

Present-Day Saints

It is not to the present purpose to analyze these arguments, or report their conclusions; but one quality, almost unique among such discussions, must be recalled. It is the lightness of touch which relieves them from ponderousness or dulness. One mark of a master is that his material does not oppress him, but can be made by him a subject for humor or irony; and this gift is so marked in Everett that his editor offers a word of apology for 'colloquial phrases which occur.' It was, however, this quality which most illuminated and transmitted the subtle thought. What argument for the freedom of the will ever before began: 'Suppose that we look at it as though we had never heard of it before'; or continued, 'Freedom of thought means the power to look facts in the face'; or illustrated freedom by the choice of paths to right or left on Cambridge Common? What evidence of the inherent excellence of human nature was ever before derived from observing 'crowds of people on a fine Sunday afternoon in winter watching the driving on the Brighton road'? What criticism of profanity was ever more unexpected than to condemn it, not so much for its wickedness as for its superficiality? 'The sin of profanity is that it indicates a superficial view of the profound relations of life.' Who that heard it can ever forget Dr. Everett's discussion of ecclesiastical claims and denominational exclusions? 'A little boy,' he said, 'sold tickets to the neighbors admit-

Charles Carroll Everett

ting them to his mother's back-yard to see the eclipse; and those who paid to come in had a good view of the event and got what they paid for; but the neighbors who stood outside the fence saw the eclipse just as well as though they were within the enclosure.' What could be the effect on a student — was it amusement or despair? — when, after listening for three hours a week through an entire year to lectures on Christian doctrine, and cramming all night from his notes for the final test, he found the entire examination announced in one little word written on the blackboard — *Sin;* and was set for three hours to cope with the problems involved? It was by such humor and vivacity that weighty discourses became enlivened; and one could almost detect in the single eye of the great scholar a furtive wink of merriment as he expounded majestic truths.

If one should inquire for justification of this light touch in dealing with grave matters, let him turn to the convincing and entertaining essay on the 'Philosophy of the Comic,' in the little volume which has been the most widely read of Everett's writings. Indeed, it may almost be said that this series of papers on 'Poetry, Comedy, and Duty,' reproduces in familiar language and literary form the principles laid down in his system of theology. Under 'Poetry' he includes the entire area of idealism, in which the philosopher finds truth and the mystic finds beauty. 'Poetry, like all art and all beauty, is the manifestation of the ideal.' 'The lover of Nature finds in the life that fills all things the love of God.' 'Love is the romance of life. It is no longer prose but poetry.' Under 'Duty,' he reconsiders the same ultimate facts of ethics which have been discussed in his 'Psychological Elements,' but in the language of an essayist, rather than that of a system-maker. 'Conscience implies something broader and larger than our individual lives. . . . The life of the spirit is weighed by something vaster than itself.' 'The path of duty is the path of life, but happy is he who can press on, sometimes laughingly and sometimes singing, along his way.'

It is not necessary to follow Dr. Everett further into the bypaths of his literary life, where he comments on authors and events with discriminating judgments and illuminating epigrams. The first impression made by his delightful essays is not of their erudition but of their mastery and ease. Argument and analysis become the instruments of a vivid imagination. His criticisms are not destructive, but suggestive, and are often the more penetrating because of their restraint. His weapon is not a club but a rapier, and this is so keen that its victim may not even be conscious of its thrust. In a word, it was permitted to a generation of students for the ministry to be guided and restrained by a character so self-effacing as never to be conspicuous, yet so convincing as to communicate both thought and

Charles Carroll Everett

life. The risk that an undenominational seminary
might become despiritualized disappeared when its
representative theologian and Dean was a spiritually
minded saint. No man ever more deserved to have
written of him the lines which Lowell dedicated to
the memory of another Harvard scholar:

'The wisest man could ask no more of fate
Than to be simple, modest, manly, true;
Safe from the many, honored by the few.
To count as naught in World or Church or State,
But inwardly, in secret, to be great.

. . . .

'He widened knowledge and escaped the praise;
He wisely taught, because more wise to learn;
He toiled for Science, not to draw men's gaze,
But for her love of self-denial stern.
That such a man could spring from our decays,
Fans the soul's nobler faith until it burn.'

CHAPTER VII

ALFRED TREDWAY WHITE

A SECOND academic venture which had both the joy and the risks of novelty was a more personal enterprise, and must always be associated with the name of Alfred Tredway White.

My affectionate intimacy with him — a closer and more confidential friendship than often occurs between grown men — was a late arrival in my experience, but soon became the most sustaining and reassuring guide of my thought and work. We were of about the same age, and were concerned with the same problems of social amelioration and reform ; but had never met each other until we were over thirty years of age, and then by what seemed an accident of professional life.

Our paths of early education lay far apart. Alfred White had been trained to be an engineer, and had received his degree, at the age of nineteen, from the Rensselaer Polytechnic Institute in Troy, New York. The demands of his family's business, however, soon made it necessary for him to attach himself to his father and uncle, and later, with his brother, to continue the title of a firm which has maintained an honorable piace in New York for nearly a century. I, on the other hand, having been forced to abandon a parish ministry and to enter the

a/fy yours

Alfred T. White

Alfred Tredway White

academic life, had in large degree lost contact with men in business affairs. In this withdrawal from preaching to teaching, it had occurred to me, however, to undertake, at first with a small group of divinity students, and in 1882 with a large section of undergraduates, some examination of the ethical problems and needs which were confronting and disturbing the modern world. It was a rash venture, and was observed by some of my colleagues with scepticism, or even with friendly derision. Professor Tucker, later the beloved President of Dartmouth College, had, one year earlier, and in the quiet precincts of Andover Seminary, offered to his students a similar course of study, concerned with the application of Christian motives to philanthropic work; but this was a distinctly professional undertaking, designed to promote among young ministers a clearer understanding of the social problems they were soon to meet. Its most notable result was the establishment of 'Andover House' in Boston, which still perpetuates as 'South End House' the influence of Dr. Tucker on his pupil, Robert Woods. The notion that such subjects might be appropriate, not merely as instruments of professional efficiency, but for the training of young men in college, as a legitimate part of a liberal education, preparing them for the world in which they were to live, was so novel that one of the most respected of Harvard professors frankly confessed that he did not see how such studies could be 'seriously pursued.'

There were certainly some considerations which seemed to encourage this distrust. Academic administrators are likely to dread innovations as disturbing the balance of studies; and here was a plan which had no precedent in any country, and was involved in many risks both from bad economics and from loose sentimentalism. There was also serious lack of scholastic material. The literature of social agitation and reform, which is now so abundant, was practically non-existent forty years ago. What is described in college as 'required reading' had to be derived either from incidental articles or from annual reports of institutions, or from the propagandist writings of precipitate reformers. Professors of economics were inclined to oppose what seemed an invasion of their field, and radical critics were disappointed by a guarded or academic treatment. A jocular cynic in the Harvard faculty described the new course as one on 'Drainage and Divorce'; and a compositor at the University Press unconsciously reached the climax of criticism by sending to the office a galley-proof of the next year's offering which announced that my instruction was to be changed from a 'half Curse' to a 'whole Curse.' Even the title descriptive of such studies was for years undetermined. At first, with some exaggeration, it was classified as 'Philosophy 5'; later it

Alfred Tredway White

was described as 'The Ethics of the Social Questions,' and finally the impulsive genius of William James suggested, 'Why not call it "Social Ethics"?' and that title was soon accepted, not only by Harvard University, but by similar courses and departments in many American colleges and universities, quite without knowledge of the fact that the name had been reached after much tentative fumbling and as a slowly realized survival of the fittest.

Thus the academic foundling, without legitimate descent from any recognized department of study, wandered from room to room, repelled by economics, tolerated by philosophy, and not quite certain itself to what family it belonged. Alfred White, observing this homelessness, said one day that what was needed in the University was a long building with two wings, housing in one the instruction in economics and in the another that in philosophy, and between the two a central dome assigned to Social Ethics, which might be entered from either end, by an economist who wanted to learn of duty, or by a philosopher who wanted to learn of economic laws. It must be added, however, that when this Cinderella was provided with a substantial dowry in her own right and was settled in a fine home, the attitude of her relations became that of competition for intimacy rather than that of condescension or indifference, and that another department candidly proposed adopting social ethics under its family name, in spite of the dubious pedigree — but with the fortune.

Inadequate and provisional as such pioneer work became, it offered an inviting challenge to a young teacher whose chief equipment was the valor of ignorance. To set one's hand to a brand new undertaking in university life, and one which the conditions of the world made timely, if not imperative, was a venture worth the risk of much academic indifference and much struggling with inadequate material; and while many youths got little from their researches but an easy 'C,' here and there, I like to believe, a life was steadied or a career determined. The most reassuring counsel I can recollect was that of a veteran in the faculty to whom I confessed my insufficient equipment, and who said: 'You must remember, my young friend, the Oriental proverb, "Among the blind a one-eyed man is king."' Throughout the arduous years of consciously experimental effort to direct these groups of young men — some of them passionately interested, some mildly tolerant, and some passively resistant — it was a solace to reflect that, dimly as I could see the way of social sanity and peace, most of those before me were almost totally blind; and the chief source of professional satisfaction in old age has been to learn, now and then, from an administrator of business or a promoter of sane reform, that his youthful researches in social ethics have given direction or momentum to his useful life.

It was in the course of this academic teaching, which might seem to have been remote from Wall Street, that lives so divergent in their interests as Alfred White's and mine at last happily met. In lecturing on the principles of poor-relief, I had been led to report the plans, then just beginning to take shape in various countries, for the provision of improved dwellings for working-people, and to call attention to the consistency of such schemes with economic stability; or, as the maxim of the new science called it, philanthropy and five per cent. The Peabody Dwellings had already been established in London, and in 1883 were housing not less than fourteen thousand persons, with so prudent a scheme of cumulative income that, when I was inspecting their admirable premises, the superintendent jestingly remarked that within a time quite within computation the entire population of the metropolis might be his tenants. Indeed, the chief obstacle met at this time by the Peabody scheme, as later by the Sage Foundation's Garden City, was the occupation of these attractive lodgings by tenants quite above the wage-earning group, who found economy consistent with reasonable comfort. In London, also, Sir Sydney Waterlow had established his Improved Dwellings Company as early as 1863, with domestic conveniences provided for each family at a rental of about two shillings a week for each room, and average net earnings of six per cent a year.

The first, and for many years the best, American illustration of this new science, combining wise philanthropy and sound business, had been given in 1876 in Brooklyn, New York, through the private initiative of Alfred White.[1] The English examples had attracted his attention when he was but twenty-nine years old, and, with the prudence of a man of affairs, he crossed the ocean, examined the system and budget of the Waterlow Buildings and other similar ventures, and, returning to Brooklyn, set himself to devise a similar plan for its rapidly growing and seriously congested population. He enlisted his family in the investment, and proceeded to erect in the thickly settled district near the docks, first the Tower Buildings, and later the Riverside Buildings, which when completed contained five hundred and forty-seven lodgings, besides thirty small houses, providing in all about two thousand tenants with every convenience of domestic seclusion, sanitary protection, fireproof construction, playgrounds for children, and a rebate of one month's rental for prompt payment throughout the year, while at the

[1] The story is told in detail in two pamphlets of Alfred White's: *Improved Dwellings for the Laboring Classes*, Putnam, 1879 (with illustrations); and *Better Homes for Workingmen*. Twelfth Nat. Conf. of Charities, 1885. See also, De Forest and Veiller, *The Tenement House Problem*, Macmillan, 1903, I, 97, 333, 364; II, 94, 95.

same time earning an annual income of six per cent on the investment. It was an unprecedented venture in this country, and opened the way to the many and more ambitious schemes of 'Tenementology' which, with varying degrees of success, have been undertaken in many American cities.

Such was the enterprise which demanded personal observation if it were to be the subject of academic lectures, and I therefore made a pilgrimage to Brooklyn, and for the first time met the founder of these dwellings, then about thirty-five years old. It was on my part a case of love at first sight, and on his part the beginning of forty years of devoted friendship. We were, by inheritance and conviction, of the same religious faith and communion, and there were few incidents in my own religious life so appealing and tranquillizing as the family worship shared in his home before the busy day's work began. He was blessed with a most lovely and devoted wife, of the same rational faith and the same complete dedication to generous thoughts and deeds, and his home life has been to many a guest a lesson in the simplicity which is in Christ. Indeed, it was more than once a matter of playful discussion among friends whether Mr. or Mrs. White was the more perfect in character — a debate which never reached a conclusive decision.

He was himself so unassuming and unimpressive, with such quietness of demeanor, that I did not for years realize his vigor of thought or strength of will. At our first meeting we walked together through his buildings, and I observed with surprise that scarcely any occupant whose home we inspected showed any sign of recognizing the landlord, who was at the same time the patron saint of the community. No taint of patronage or charity had been felt; the administration had become so automatic and business-like, and the occupant so personally concerned, through an expected dividend, for the maintenance of cleanliness and order, that the merits of the buildings were proudly exhibited to the visiting strangers as the occupant's possession. Philanthropy had been completely submerged in efficiency; the owner was disguised as a guest.

From this point of contact, and through many experiences of companionship, both in his home and mine, of excursions in summer and conversations in winter, I came by degrees to know something of other doings of this unassuming and chivalric friend, some of which may be briefly recapitulated. In 1878, with his cousin Seth Low and other young citizens of Brooklyn, he had founded the Bureau of Charities, and was its president for thirty years. To this charge were soon added official relations with almost every beneficent project of his city, its Children's Aid Society, its Society for the Prevention of Cruelty to Children, its care of the blind; and, with peculiar affection, its establishment of a botanical garden, where the lovely Japanese section is a memorial of his munificence. He was one of the original trustees of the Sage Foundation, and a member of the first executive committee of the American Red Cross, as organized for the World War; he was decorated by the King of Serbia in recognition of his gifts to that country; and received from the King of Belgium the Order of the Cross. The Polytechnic Institute at Troy, Smith College, the District Nursing Association of Brooklyn, Tuskegee and Hampton Institutes, and many other institutions, were reënforced by his gifts. From 1893 to 1895 he served as Commissioner of Public Works for Brooklyn, incurring the bitter hostility of certain contractors by his resolute defiance of their schemes; but on his withdrawal receiving an emblazoned testimonial from the very men who had opposed him, commending his integrity and foresight. In recognition of his judicious philanthropy, Harvard University, in 1890, conferred on him the honorary degree of Master of Arts, accompanying it with words so sonorous — for degrees were still given in Latin — that a translation would be an act of impiety: '*Alfredum Tredway White:* — *Virum recte divitem esse scientem, tectorum ad usum operariorum designatorem callidum, dominum beneficum.*' These and many other forms of public service and private beneficence made him universally regarded as the first citizen of Brooklyn; and his death, in 1921, was the occasion of a memorial meeting at the Academy of Music, where rich and poor, black and white, Catholics and Protestants, with beautiful unanimity of affection, testified to a sense of bereavement which few private citizens have ever inspired.

The circumstances of his death increased this sense of calamity. Nothing had given him so much refreshment, after a week in Wall Street, as a day among the solitudes of Nature, where he might lift up his eyes to the hills for help. With this desire for release, he had set out on a Saturday in January for a tramp among the mountains of the Ramapo Range, west of the Hudson River, and was skating alone on one of the numerous lakes when he broke through the ice and was drowned. The disaster was a startling shock to the whole community; but as one reflects more calmly it may be felt that sudden death, coming to a man of seventy-five years, in the fulness of athletic vigor, and with an unbroken record of integrity and beneficence, cannot be regarded as deplorable. He died without anticipation or prolonged suffering, in the midst of the wild nature where his physical renewal had always been sought and found, and mourned by a whole city and by grateful friends in many lands.

These public acts of citizenship and benevolence are, however, not the most convincing evidence of Alfred White's character. By degrees, and often by accident, I became aware of a long series of private and often anonymous benefactions, in which he had found peculiar happiness, and in which his wife had shared with all the sympathy of her beautiful soul. When, for example, at the beginning of the World War, the towns of Belgium had been devastated, and before any organization of relief had been proposed in this country, Cardinal Mercier's representative received each month a substantial sum, transmitted through a Belgian priest in Brooklyn, from givers who described themselves as 'friends.' The Cardinal took from his own study table a precious crucifix and ordered it transmitted to these anonymous friends, who had anticipated the general sense of sympathy and compassion which this country soon expressed. On arriving in America Cardinal Mercier learned for the first time the names of these friends, and forthwith invited Mr. and Mrs. White to a private audience, and gave his gracious blessing to these American Unitarians. When, again, a messenger reached this country bringing the sad news of desperate need among the Unitarian Churches in Transylvania under Rumanian rule, he was led to inquire the source of a series of generous gifts which had been anonymously sent to these stricken congregations; and discovered that they proceeded from one family in Brooklyn, where the need had been recognized and met before it had been generally appreciated or relieved.

Of these unprompted benefactions, one of the most surprising was his reënforcement and endowment of the teaching which, with such imperfect equipment and slight encouragement, I had been trying to give. Alfred had often expressed his sympathy with my undertaking, and remarked one day that his own way in social service might have been less hard to find if he had been given earlier guidance. One morning, at his home, as we sat by the fire after breakfast before departing to our different duties, he inquired in a casual manner what would seem to me the best way to help young men like himself to care for the social problems which made the subjects of my lectures. It had been necessary, he said, for him to cross the ocean to learn the science of housing; might not other young men be taught while yet in college how to use their time and means effectively for the public good?

It happened that at the moment the Department of Philosophy at Harvard was pledged to the plan of a special building, and had received only two thirds of the one hundred and fifty thousand dollars necessary for the purpose. I replied, therefore, that I thought the teaching of social ethics would be most assured of its future if a permanent place could be secured for it in Emerson Hall; and a few days later Alfred White astonished the department by subscribing the necessary fifty thousand dollars, with the condition that pro-rata space should be assigned to instruction in social ethics. As a consequence, the greater part of the second floor of Emerson Hall

Alfred Tredway White

was thus secured, with space not only for lecture-rooms but for a special library and for a 'Social Museum' — a collection of designs, charts, and illustrations of social work which it had been my dream to provide. 'I believe,' he wrote in his letter of gift, 'that the interest in the study of the social questions will broaden if the facilities for such studies be increased, and I should be glad to aid in making such provision at Harvard as may perpetuate, expand, and dignify the course already established. . . . This contribution is to be entered for the present simply as from a contributor to the Study of the Ethics of the Social Questions, and my name is not to be published in connection with it without my consent hereafter.'

President Eliot's reply to this characteristic letter contains the following paragraph : 'Perhaps you do not fully understand the happiness you are preparing for him [Professor Peabody]. When a man has through long years built up a body of university instruction, invented its methods, interested the students in it, and accumulated with difficulty an incomplete special library, and all the time has had very little assistance and no mechanical and clerical aids, he dreads to grow old, lest his work should not be continued and developed by competent successors; lest in short it prove to be personal and temporary instead of institutional and permanent. What you are proposing to do — as I understand it

147

— will make Professor Peabody's work on the ethical dealing with the grave social and industrial evils which beset our American communities permanent at Harvard University.'

Alfred's appetite for giving being thus stimulated, he proceeded, without suggestion or knowledge of mine — indeed, during my absence on a sabbatical half-year — to fortify the work with an endowment of one hundred thousand dollars, followed by various gifts for furnishings, for the library, and for scholarships; and finally, at his death, by a bequest of one hundred thousand dollars. His total gifts thus reached at least three hundred thousand dollars; and the instruction which for years had been only that of an individual, and had been driven from one lecture-room to another without assurance of permanence, became established as a distinct department and recognized unit in the University.

The appointment, in 1920, of the distinguished teacher and physician, Dr. Richard C. Cabot, as my successor, gave to social ethics a new importance in the college curriculum, and under the direction of his fertile genius there were serving in the department in 1926 a staff of two professors, eight instructors and other officers, offering more than twenty courses of instruction, with three hundred and sixty registered students, and a special library of more than six thousand volumes for their use. For more than ten years the gifts which have made this growth

possible were, as has been indicated, entered as
anonymous, and it was not until a new professor
took command of the department that the source
of this stream of generosity was discovered to be,
not a graduate of Harvard, but an unsuspected, and
to most Harvard men an unknown, benefactor. His
motive is sufficiently shown in a letter to President
Lowell in 1917 : 'While I sympathize with the desire
to provide instruction especially designed for Divinity School students, I also keep in mind the interests
of that large body of undergraduates who are likely
to become men of affairs, and who should realize
the fundamentally ethical nature of many of our
social problems.'

Nor must it be inferred that the gifts thus
described were of money alone. An even more sustaining contribution was the complete understanding and sympathy with which Alfred White watched
the experimental years of this new type of study.
The somewhat slender support secured within the
College Staff was more than compensated for by the
approval of a man of that world which social ethics
was to interpret and serve. It has seldom happened
that two men of such different traditions have found
themselves thinking and planning with such unconstrained identity of hope and faith ; and after years of
silence I find myself asking, at almost every point of
personal or national decision, how Alfred's mind would
have dealt with the case and have shown the way.

Present=Day Saints

These reminiscences of a beloved friend tempt one to some reflections on the uses of wealth, and the place of rich men under the conditions of the modern world. No thoughtful person can disguise from himself the fact that the so-called capitalistic system which fortifies private ownership is in an unstable condition and as yet on trial. Agitators and revolutionists affirm that it degrades the possessors and wrongs the dispossessed; and there are instances enough of the misuse or waste of surplus capital to encourage the advocates of confiscation or of communal control. The trouble with the rich often seems to be, not that they have money, but that they do not know what to do with it. They have learned to get, but they have not learned to use. The development of the prehensile grasp has involved an atrophy of the open palm. The only use of money which has become congenial is to make more. Their wealth has become what Ruskin called their 'ill-th'; it is not well but ill with them, and the more wealth they accumulate the more they provoke protest and justify revolution.

A life like Alfred White's — modest, sagacious, and discriminating, — thus provides the best defence that can be offered for the present system of industry. A rich man who regards himself not as a possessor but as a trustee, who is conscious of owing his wealth as much as of owning it, is more likely to be judicious and far-seeing in his benefactions than the schemes of politicians or the judgments of less competent men. The same discretion is likely to be applied to giving which has been used in getting, and the world is better, not only for the money received, but for the sagacity with which it is distributed. In other words, the system of private ownership, instead of being, as it is often supposed to be, easy to administer, is a stern test of character. It calls for conscience as well as for capacity. Cupidity is often an evidence of stupidity. Ownership involves obligation. Service is the only way to freedom. A rich man may be worth having, if he use his peculiar facilities for benefiting society. The capitalist may be the most economical agent which the community can employ. The system of private capital which may be so easily misused offers the best of opportunities for magnanimity and wisdom; but if, on the other hand, self-aggrandizement and vulgar ostentation shall supplant simplicity and self-sacrifice as the habit of the prosperous, the capitalistic system — now under severe strain — is likely to be found wanting and to be displaced.

The future of wealth is thus in its own hands, and the most active promoters of social revolution are those who abuse the privilege of private ownership. To meet this test, to live with simplicity, and hold one's life and property as trusts for the common good, is to justify the language of President Eliot in conferring the honorary degree on Alfred White, and to know how to be 'nobly rich.' 'How hardly shall they that have riches,' said Jesus, 'enter into the kingdom of God!' Yes, but when they do come in, having passed the barriers of their indolence and self-indulgence, it may be that the gates are lifted up as for a hard-won victory. The man of whom Jesus demanded the great renunciation : 'Sell that thou hast, and give to the poor, and thou shalt have treasure in heaven, and come and follow me!' was one who had 'great possessions,' yet Jesus 'beholding him loved him,' and it may have been that though he was 'sad at that saying, and went away grieved,' the loving look of Jesus followed him, and made what seemed his cross become in the end his crown.

To justify this way of life, however, more is needed than good intentions. The administration of wealth as a trust calls for personal qualities quite as rare as those which insure the acquisition of wealth. Distribution may be as profitless as hoarding. Investment in philanthropy calls for as much prudence as investment in securities. Most givers of money wait until, among the multitudinous calls for their aid, their contribution becomes compulsory ; the demand is thrust upon them and they surrender. The wise distributor of wealth, on the contrary, must have a faculty of prevision. Precisely as the maker of money anticipates needs and foresees the course of events, so the giver of money, if he is to invest it profitably, must be endowed with a constructive imagination which reënforces sagacity by foresight. His success, like that of the enterprising financier, is in developing unsuspected resources and meeting unrecognized wants. He must exhibit the same qualities of venturesomeness and originality which make other people rich. Like Wordsworth's Happy Warrior, he

'Through the heat of conflict, keeps the law
In calmness made, and sees what he foresaw.'

He adds to generosity prevision; he has not only an open hand but an open mind.

A still rarer trait in the wise use of wealth is persistency. Much giving, even by generous people, is occasional, spasmodic, and transitory. An object is temporarily interesting; but the giver soon passes to the next benefaction. It is said that the average duration of loyalty to a relief association is not more than five years. The enterprises which Alfred White directed and reënforced are perhaps most of all indebted to him for an indomitable persistency. Having once assumed an obligation, no vicissitude disheartened him and no reverse made his devotion slacken. It was one thing to organize a Bureau of Charities in Brooklyn, but quite another thing to watch each detail of administration, and refresh an exhausted treasury during a term of thirty years. It was an interesting venture to endow a Department of Social Ethics; but it was a much severer test of character to be the anonymous source of a continuous stream of benefactions for twenty years, and to secure their continuance after death. To take up with new causes is exhilarating; but to maintain causes where romance has been lost in routine calls for the rarer gift of persistency. *'Justum et tenacem propositi virum'* — the praise which Horace gave to his ideal statesman — might have been written of Alfred White. The just man holds on to whatever he undertakes.

These gifts of prevision and persistency, which made Alfred White a permanent example in the administration of wealth, were fortified and sustained by a still more commanding habit of mind. It was his rational and lifelong faith in the Divine guidance of the individual and of the world. The supreme lesson of his beautiful life was that of worldly wisdom derived from unworldly consecration. It was the wisdom which is from above, and which is first pure, then peaceable, full of mercy and good fruits. Behind a manner of sunny and unassuming kindliness which made him a delightful companion were the firmness and serenity derived from the habitual dedication of his life to accomplish, not his own will but the will of Him who sent him. His religious life was uncomplicated and serene. Neither domestic sorrow nor public controversy could disturb his tranquillity or self-control. He directed his daily efforts as ever in his Great Taskmaster's eye. It was this habit of faith which led him to works of love. His social service was the corollary of his Christian consecration. His generosity was the natural flower of a deep-rooted and daily-watered religious life. The secret of his beneficent activity was in his early discovery and continual assurance of the life of God in the soul of man. Religious faith, in short, for one thus concerned with social service, is not a super-added luxury but a fundamental support. The interpretation of the imperfect task is in the conviction of the perfect law. The escape from mechanism and routine is in the freedom of faith. Serenity and detachment are reserved for those who have entered into the communion of the saints.

I cherish the happy memory of spending with Alfred White the last evening of his life. A lovely daughter, in recalling whose character her friends instinctively used the word 'radiant,' had served untiringly in Washington during the World War, and being stricken by disease was too war-worn to resist it, and died as truly in the ranks as though she were killed in a trench at the front. Knowing her keen interest in Hampton Institute, her husband caused an inviting club-house to be built there on the water-front, and her father equipped this delightful meeting place with furniture, with a fleet of canoes for the use of the devoted teachers, and with an endowment for its maintenance. We were to dedicate this 'Katharine House,' as it was later called, on a Sunday in January, 1921, and I proceeded to Hampton to await Alfred's arrival, only to hear on Sunday morning of his tragic death, and to have the sorrowing assemblage meet with the Virginian sunshine overshadowed by a mist of tears. This last expression of his generosity — and none was more scrupulously studied in every detail of convenience and charm — was a touching symbol of his self-effacing life. It was enough if he might reënforce his son-in-law's affectionate intention, and perpetuate in grateful memory, not his own name, but that of his radiant child.

> 'Whom does the Master choose to be his friend?
> Whom does he trust his wandering flock to tend?
> Not him whose creed is longest, or whose praise
> Echoes the certitudes of other days;
> But the trained leader in the world's fierce strife,
> Whose faith is service and whose worship life;
> Whose lavish heart serves with far-seeing eyes,
> Whose truth is mercy, and whose pity wise;
> To whom possessions make an open door
> To save the city and to serve the poor;
> Whose monuments of unrecorded good
> Escape the praises of the multitude;
> For whom the city's sterile wilderness
> Blossoms with homes amid its homelessness;
> And from the deadening tumult of the street
> The fragrant garden tempts the toiler's feet.
> Across the ages speaks the Son of Man:
> "For such God's kingdom waits since time began;
> This, which ye do so self-effacingly
> Unto these least, ye do it unto me." '

CHAPTER VIII

PHILLIPS BROOKS

I PASS to the third, and the most important, undertaking in university life with which
I have had the happiness to be associated, and
which owed a great part of its permanence and
effectiveness to the confident leadership of Phillips
Brooks.

Here, however, I write with less claim to intimacy
than in the case of Carroll Everett or of Alfred White.
Shortly after the death of Phillips Brooks, a clerical
brother, in eulogizing the Bishop, described himself
as 'an intimate friend of Phillips Brooks,' but George
Gordon, who had as good a right to that title as any
one, remarked, 'None of us has a right to say that
he was intimate with Phillips Brooks.' There was,
in other words, within a fraternal, and even playful,
manner, an inner life of isolated experience which
revealed itself only in rare moments of sympathy;
and more frequently, as is not unusual in preachers,
through the message of the pulpit than through candor in conversation. One could go a long way with
Phillips Brooks in affectionate banter or frank discussion; but would forfeit all claim to friendship
if conversation became inquisitive or impertinent.
Those who knew him best knew that there was much
in him which they did not know. Yet this sense of a

hidden life only deepened the reverence with which one found himself admitted, as it were, to its outer courts, but was aware of a holy of holies which few might enter.

The story of Phillips Brooks's life has been told, perhaps with too unrestrained completeness, in the monumental biography by his devoted friend Professor Allen; and his unparalleled distinction among the preachers of his generation has been repeatedly described by many observers in many lands. When, however, in 1886, he endorsed the plan of abolishing compulsory attendance at worship in Harvard University, and enlisted in the first Staff of Preachers for the administration of voluntary worship, this new enterprise permitted a close and confidential companionship; and, as the administrator of its details, I was admitted, not indeed to intimacy, but to the privilege of receiving his untiring coöperation and sustaining friendship. I may therefore with confidence recall this single point in his great career.

The origin of this venture of faith, which has now become so institutionalized as to need no defence, is of interest as an evidence of Phillips Brooks's courage and candor. There had been for some years signs of restlessness among our undergraduates, and several waves of protest against compulsion had swept up from the students upon the governing boards. The system, they urged, with somewhat

Ever faithfully Yours

Phillips Brooks

Phillips Brooks

boyish ferocity, was 'a remnant of ancient encroachments upon civil liberty, and therefore tyrannical and unjust.' [1]

In 1885, therefore, a committee of three, of which Phillips Brooks was a member, was appointed by the Board of Overseers to consider these urgent petitions. This committee reported that a change of method was inexpedient and likely to involve the disappearance of daily religious services. 'Harvard College can ill afford the loss of reputation which would ensue on its being the first of all literary institutions in New England to abandon religious observances.' This negative report was endorsed by a majority of the Board of Overseers, including, it is said, so improbable a supporter as Ralph Waldo Emerson. When, however, after the Plummer professorship, with the administration of the Chapel, had been reluctantly declined by Phillips Brooks, and my appointment to this responsibility was under consideration, I found myself wholly concurring with the view of the undergraduates that compulsory attendance at worship was, as they said, 'repugnant.' It seemed to me, on the other hand, possible that the necessary transition might be so made as to be not a retreat but an advance, and that liberty in worship might reënforce rather than defeat its influence. I therefore wrote to Phillips

[1] The progress of the discussion is reported in detail in A. V. G. Allen's *Life and Letters of Phillips Brooks*, 1900, II, 613-18.

Brooks, as a member of the Board of Overseers, the following letter :

March 21, 1886

MY DEAR SIR :

To any one who cares about religion and about Harvard College the vote of the Overseers this week is a matter of great concern, and I will not apologize for offering even the least contribution to the question.

It seems plain that the time has come for a great transition. The dogma of the University is now 'Discipline through liberty.' Under this method the old customs of worship are near extinction. Sunday worship is driven from morning to evening, and from the whole year to less than half ; and Prayers are likely soon to be a 'survival.' If the Overseers simply vote to abandon the present method of Prayers, they are taking the last step in secularization, and a step which cannot be retraced. But, on the other hand, they may so make the transition that the change shall be not a surrender but an advance. Instead of eliminating religious life, they may so magnify its office that the question of method of Prayers shall be subordinated. If there could be in the University a healthy movement of religious interest, then one need not fear the fate of the voluntary method. The main duty, therefore, as it seems to me, of the Overseers, is to make this change a change forward, so that they shall not seem to retreat from religion, but shall develop the present unsatisfactory ways into more living ones. To this end, they should, in my judgment, proceed thus:

1. They should postpone action on the Prayers petition until it can be developed into a larger scheme.

2. They should demand that the administration of religion be magnified into the work of a department. A department in Harvard University means a staff of from three to six men, and an expenditure of from ten thousand dollars to twenty thousand dollars a year. The work of the University is now done by departments. Members of this staff act in concert and for the good of the department. A slight beginning in the direction of a department has been already made in religion through the coöperation of eight men in the conduct of Prayers. It is this same method which should now be thoroughly attempted.

3. The organization of this department should be in plan like that of a large English church. There should be:

(a) A permanently resident minister, who should be the administrator of the department, as a Dean administers a church.

(b) A staff, not of assistants, but of coadjutors, who should take their turn in service, as Canons succeed each other in a church. These persons should be officially appointed, as lecturers and professors are appointed, by the Board of Overseers.

They should be during their term within reach as pastors. They should be of different denominations. They should confer with each other for connected work throughout the year. They should be well paid, as for a position of high honor and responsibility.

4. This departmental body may accomplish work like the following :

(a) Sunday evening worship throughout the year.

(b) Voluntary daily Prayers.

(c) Week-day afternoon vesper service with music.

(d) Sunday afternoon instruction in religious and social duty.

(e) The provision of a Board of Advisers for students, through an hour and a place where they may be found.

Varied and active work like this cannot be accomplished by one man. Nor is it well that one man should represent religion in the University. In such enlargement of duty the present problem becomes insignificant.

Very truly yours,

Francis G. Peabody

What was my surprise a few days later, when I was lecturing to a handful of students in Divinity Hall, to see the giant form of Dr. Brooks in the doorway ! He had studied my letter with care, and had found in the plan proposed a way out of his dilemma. At the next meeting of the Board of Overseers he announced his complete conversion to a comprehensive scheme, which should be introduced 'not as a concession but as the ideal arrangement.' 'There was,' his biographer says, 'surprise, and even astonishment, at the complete reversal of his attitude'; but he warmly maintained that the plan should be adopted 'because of its inherent fitness and propriety.' My appointment as Plummer Professor was thereupon confirmed, and a Staff of Preachers was designated, consisting of Edward Everett Hale, Alexander MacKenzie, Phillips Brooks, George A. Gordon, and a young Baptist, Richard Montague, who was prevented by ill health from serving. Reverend William R. Huntington was invited to join the first Staff, but after careful consideration concluded that this added task was inconsistent with his many parochial obligations. It was a serious disappointment to fail in this case, and opened the question whether the University could fairly expect to command the service of the busiest and most effective preachers. It has been no small satisfaction, therefore, to observe that during the thirty years of my administration no other minister, when summoned to this duty, has found himself able to decline the invitation. Most of them would have concurred with the reply which Dr. Lyman Abbott gave to the call. It was, he said, one that it was almost impossible to accept, but entirely impossible to decline.

Present-Day Saints

These four Preachers, with the Plummer Professor, made it their first duty to transmit to the President and Fellows of the University the following votes:

June 8, 1886

'The Plummer Professor and the Preachers to the University, as appointed for the year 1886–87, have conferred concerning the work of that year, and desire to make to the Corporation the following recommendations:

'1. We recommend that in Statute 15, concerning religious services, the clause "at which the attendance of the students is required" be stricken out.

'2. It is our intention to hold daily prayers and Sunday evening worship throughout the academic year, and also an afternoon vesper service once a week during a part of the year. We therefore recommend that an increased appropriation be made for music in the College Chapel.'

June 29, 1886

'At a meeting of the Plummer Professor and the Preachers to the University as appointed for the year 1886–87, held June 28, 1886, it was

'Voted, That the Corporation and Overseers be recommended to make such alteration in Statute XIII (concerning the Parietal committee) as shall free the Parietal committee from the obligation of attending Daily Prayers.'

Phillips Brooks

In acknowledging the receipt of these recommendations, President Eliot, with characteristic loyalty, replied : 'Whatever measures the Board may propose I intend to support.'

The first of these votes transferred the responsibility for liberty from the students to the Preachers, and made the new system, not a surrender to petitions, but a condition of service. The second, and hardly less welcome, vote emancipated those professors and tutors who occupied rooms in the College Yard from the repulsive duty of supervising decorum during daily worship. It is difficult at this distance to realize the sense of a new moral order which thus ensued when it was announced that the worship of God in Harvard University would be henceforth administered without penalties and without police.

The new plan was launched in September, 1886, at a religious service in which all the Preachers took part. There was no lack, it must be said, of scepticism, both in the college staff and in the community, concerning so unprecedented a venture. The Preachers, on the other hand, applied themselves to their task with confidence, meeting frequently for conference, kneeling together in prayer for guidance, and scrutinizing each detail of administration. Each Preacher accepted duty for four Sunday evenings during the college year and for the intervening five weeks of daily Prayers, detaching himself for this considerable term from his pastoral duties or professional cares. Daily worship was enriched by the addition of a full choir of men and boys, supplanting the meagre music of an unpaid and uninstructed choir of students. A new hymn book and a book of readings were compiled adapted to the needs of young men. Special services were arranged for Thursday afternoons, and attracted large numbers of listeners ; and a collection of the brief addresses there delivered was published under the title 'Harvard Vespers.' A Preachers' Room was established in the venerable house of the early Presidents of the University, and there on each morning during his term of service the preacher was at home to students, often for paternal or fraternal conversation, but not infrequently for interviews so intimate and searching as to make the Preachers' Room a confessional.

Phillips Brooks's letters indicate the enthusiasm and confidence with which he himself undertook this new and onerous duty. Thus, when the first service under the new plan was contemplated, he wrote :

' DEAR MR. PEABODY, —

' I feel very strongly, as I think about it, that the meeting of October 3d should be devoted to a full and comprehensive address from you, for which you should take plenty of time, and in which you should lay before the College and the world the complete meaning of the new movement. If it is thought well for one of the preachers to say a few words also, well and good. . . . Let us not fail to get a great musician ; and we must not be cramped for money ; and we must be very confident in hope.'

And again on August 18 : 'I hope that the service may be as rich and strong as it is possible to make it. I have begged the President that we may not be stinted in the matter of money. At any rate, for those two days let there be no economy. Get the best musical material that can be had. Put our musical director on his mettle, regardless of expense, and let us see what he can do ; only let him know that it is excellence of quality, and not simply abundance of quantity, that we want.'

And yet once more, at the end of his first weeks of service : 'I cannot tell you how much I have enjoyed this last busy month, or how deeply interested I am in the world over which you preside. Pray use me for it in any way at any time, and do not let even Cambridge quench your hope.'

It was this indomitable faith that insured to the new plan its stability and momentum. It was Phillips Brooks who first added to the short service of morning prayers a brief address, which soon became a regular and precious enrichment. For five weeks of each busy winter, during a term of five years, he lavished his time and thought on this superadded

service, with painstaking concern for each detail and
studied thought for each life which sought his counsel. Nothing could exhaust the magnanimity and
considerateness with which he demanded the right
on various occasions to assist, rather than to lead,
in worship, and the sympathy with which he attended
services of worship conducted by others of the staff.
There is one pew in the College Chapel where an
intrusive pillar cuts off the corner and leaves a vacant
space. Phillips Brooks discovered here room enough
for his long legs, and his figure is still seen there in
retrospect by a few surviving colleagues, stretched
out in animated and childlike attention to the words
of less gifted men.

As one thus recalls this unique personality — as
majestic in spirit as in form — one's first impression
is, of course, of his transcendent and compelling
power as a preacher. He was beyond question one
of the great preachers of Christian history, to be
ranked with Chrysostom and Bossuet, with Schleiermacher and Robertson; and nowhere was he more
convincing and searching than in the chapel of the
College which he so deeply loved. 'This is the greatest of preaching-places,' he once said; and he brought
to us not only an untiring and generous service,
but a peculiar and conscious joy.

His preaching was in its form very different from
that of other masters. In spite of a wonderful gift
of free speech his University sermons were invariably

Phillips Brooks

written and read from manuscript, with scarcely a gesture except the lifting of the eyes and the grasp of the hand on the gown. Nothing could be more remote from his pulpit method than the statue which represents him with uplifted arm in an attitude of exhortation. Restraint, passion in control, the communication of truth and beauty in absolute lucidity and purity — all these made the name of orator quite inappropriate for him. Yet the speed and rush of thought swept over us like a huge wave, lifting us on its crest, and bearing us at last to a safe shore of faith which we had hardly hoped to reach. It was one of the greatest of homiletical miracles that a way of preaching which might seem to restrict or obstruct became a way of uninterrupted and consummate inspiration. A distinguished Scotch scholar, Professor Bruce of Glasgow University, heard three sermons from Phillips Brooks on one Sunday, in New York, and when asked how the preacher compared with the great Scotch divines, said: 'They take into the pulpit a bucketful, or half-full, of the Word of God, and pump it out to the congregation; but this man is a great water-main, attached to the everlasting reservoir of truth, and a stream of life pours through him by heavenly gravitation to refresh weary souls.'

It is sometimes fancied that a man with so great a gift of swift and noble utterance is likely to trust to the occasion for his ideas, and to become an extemporaneous speaker. One of the great lessons which companionship with Phillips Brooks taught was that his genius was in large part the faculty of taking infinite pains. What seemed an inspiration of the moment was often the product of long reflection and gradual ripening. On one wintry morning at Wadsworth House, for example, he opened in conversation a subject of general interest, and it occurred to me to note when it might take shape in some public address. It was not until the following June, in a baccalaureate sermon, that the thought reappeared. For five or six months it had been lying in the soil of his mind, growing into symmetry and beauty, until at last it broke into a perfect flower of speech.

One of the most striking evidences of this apparently spontaneous eloquence, which was in fact the fruit of serious study, was in his address, in 1890, to the members of the Shoe and Leather Trade in Boston. One can fancy those prosperous and portly merchants, sitting back after their ample banquet, awaiting an after-dinner speech from Phillips Brooks, and their astonishment when he lifted their commonplace trade into idealism and beauty, and sent them home with a feeling that they were poets and artists, though they knew it not. 'Every business,' he said, 'touches the imagination. It stands between nature and man. Behind the carpenter is the waving forest; behind the factory, the sunny cotton field; behind your business, the lowing herd, the rush of buffaloes, the bleating of flocks, and the cattle upon a thousand hills.' 'What a fine business is ours!' they must have said to themselves, 'and what a wonderful speaker is this who can originate such thoughts on his feet!' Not till Phillips Brooks died, and his little note-books were examined, did it prove that he had wrought out this paragraph, pen in hand, and that what seemed a flash of genius was in reality the result of scrupulous and conscientious work.

To this impression, received by all who thronged to hear him, and who listened with bated breath, must be added the more personal traits of temperament and character which his colleagues were permitted to observe. There are many lives which look great at a distance but which shrink as one approaches them, and sees their foibles, of vanity or littleness of soul. The finest test of character is in the unguarded relations of friendship, and this undesigned effect of nobility and charm was what we most prized in Phillips Brooks. I have already recalled the remark of an observant listener, that each University preacher had a distinctive word which marked his message. Dr. Brooks's word, she said, was 'Richness.' The richness of experience, the wealth of opportunity, the prodigality of Providence — these were the fertilizing ideas which he flung down from our pulpit, as a sower flings his seed, without stint or measure, out of the abundance which he bears in his breast. One day he came into Wadsworth House and said : 'I am going to England this Spring, and have been looking over some sermons to take with me ; but I find that I have only one sermon.' Nothing could be farther from an effect of monotony than the diversity and originality of his themes ; but in a certain sense he was right ; for almost every sermon touched the same note of 'richness' and made life larger and nobler than it had been before. If he could have but one text, it would perhaps have been the great words, 'Because I live, ye shall live also' ; or, possibly, the beginning of his own sermon at our two hundred and fiftieth anniversary — 'Jesus Christ, the same yesterday, and to-day, and forever.'

No reminiscence of this academic relationship would be complete without mention of the humor, sometimes deepening into irony or satire, with which Dr. Brooks illuminated our conversations and relieved the strain of work. When we conferred at the outset on the question of possible numbers at morning chapel, some one suggested that we ought to expect a hundred ; whereupon Phillips Brooks remarked, 'If fifty young men gather in that chapel each morning, it will be the largest daily Protestant congregation in Christendom.' He was, no doubt, aware that a slight fallacy lurked behind this gallant affirmation ; for the number of Protestant congregations which gather at 8:45 A.M. daily is extremely limited. Yet the more sanguine expectation of a hundred worshippers was more than realized, and our anxious minds were amply reassured. Again, on being asked whether a certain day in the Spring would meet his convenience, he consulted his memorandum book, and said, 'That will depend on when the chairman of this Board fixes the date of Easter.' At another gathering of our Staff he excused himself from a certain duty because it was to be on Saint Bartholomew's Day; and one of his colleagues rashly asked: 'What can you preach about on Saint Bartholomew's Day? You know nothing whatever about him; he is a mere name in the Gospels.' In a flash, Phillips Brooks replied: 'That is our great homiletical opportunity! We preach on the significance of the insignificant man'; and any one who recalls his sermon on the man with two talents knows what that gospel of the insignificant man may mean.

A further trait which those who served with him cherish in memory was the complete self-subordination and genuine humility with which he joined in this work. It did not, apparently, occur to him that its effectiveness was because he was sustaining it, or that his place was at its head. When several of the Staff were proposing to share in the conduct of a service, he smilingly expressed his wish to be assigned 'to give out the hymns'; and one day he wrote in our book of private records that his term had been less fruitful in personal talks because Lyman Abbott had just preceded him, and the students had naturally sought the wiser friend.

A deeper note of character was struck in Phillips Brooks's conduct of worship. I have always regretted that his morning prayers were not written down by some hearer, though it would have needed a very expert stenographer to hold the rushing tide of petition that swept over our hearts. The conduct of free prayer is subject to many abuses; it may be superficial or impertinent or dull; yet at its best it is the highest exercise open to the human reason and the purest expression of character and consecration. Phillips Brooks's prayers at morning chapel were thus the supreme disclosure of his inner life. He began, as a rule, with a collect, repeated at tremendous speed, and then, as if on the wings of an eagle, he mounted into the great free spaces of praise and joy. It is safe to say that no worshipper there ever heard anything like it before, or will ever hear anything like it again.

Perhaps the finest illustration of this supreme gift was on the touching occasion of a student's death. A youth named Adelbert Shaw, a country lad who had won his way to great popularity, and was rowing on the University crew, was drowned in the river; and while his funeral was going on in Central New York, a memorial service was held in our chapel, and Phillips Brooks led the thronging audience of students in prayer. It was a most extraordinary

Phillips Brooks

idealization of the old-fashioned descriptive petition which was once common in New England. We saw the child in his mother's arms; we watched him working his way through school and college, loving and beloved, and at last we committed him to the care of God, as though heaven and home were not far apart.

Such, in brief outline, is the impression made on one devoted colleague by this supreme interpreter of the religious life. To great numbers of eager listeners there has never been any other voice which so convincingly and authoritatively announced the way to God and the message of Jesus Christ. I have heard critics say that there was something lacking in Phillips Brooks's preaching because he did not reach down far enough into the region of penitence, contrition, and despair. 'He did not,' one pious woman said, 'make me feel enough of a sinner.' That certainly was not his way of appeal; he spoke, not to the worst in one, but to the best. It was said of his Master that he was sent not to condemn the world but that the world through him might be saved. The same might be said of Phillips Brooks — not condemnation, but salvation, or spiritual health, was his message; not conviction of sin, but persuasion to holiness; and this message of vitality and power was conveyed, not by eloquence alone, but by the sense of a majestic unity of body, mind, and will, which gave spiritual momentum and control.

The last sermon which he preached in the Chapel of Harvard University was a perfect summary of his message to the world. Its text was the sublime promise — which, by an impressive coincidence, was Dr. Hale's last theme also — 'I am come that they might have life, and that they might have it more abundantly.' 'Friends, if there is any place in the world where that vision of the perfected life of man ought to be most real and vivid, it seems to me that it is here. I say it in all soberness. If there are any men in the world who ought to be able easily to renew the consciousness of God's Chosen People, and be sure that God has given them the privilege of setting forth His purposes and making known His will, it is these men who gather in these halls of thought and study, to begin another year of the life of the old beloved college.

'"I am come to you, here where men have dreaded and said that I could not come. I am come to you here that you may live, that you may have life and ever have it more abundantly." So speaks the Christ to the student. And with great trust and great hope and happy soberness, giving himself into the power of whatever is diviner than himself, believing truth, rejoicing in duty, the student goes forward into ever-deepening life. Of such life, and of brave, earnest men entering into its richness, may this new year of the old college life be full.'

With this message as his bequest, the body of this

goes forward into Eve. deepening life's

Of such life & of have earnest new

entering into its widenew way - the new

year of this OD College life to follow

1. Appleton Chapel, Harvard University, July 6 - Oct 4, '85!

Phillips Brooks

apostle of the abundant life was borne through the College yard to its resting-place, and the mourning throngs which lined the paths were sustained by the same sense of gratitude which led the psalmist to write, 'Blessed in the sight of the Lord is the death of his saints.'

CHAPTER IX

SAMUEL CHAPMAN ARMSTRONG

I TURN, in this series of reminiscences, from the experiences of academic life to the wider associations which have rescued that life from isolation, and have enriched it by companionship with great souls dedicated to the service of the modern world.

It was the singularly good fortune of a teacher of social ethics to be concerned with subjects which involved contact with practical schemes of social reform and industrial experiment; and I was led to make several journeys to Europe to learn at first hand how such undertakings were prospering there, — once to meet the coöperators of England and to attend their Congress; again to examine welfare-work in France and Belgium; and yet again to observe the progress of social amelioration in Germany and Switzerland. Excursions and explorations of this nature extended the range of acquaintance, and, I hope, gave some freshness and concreteness to instruction.

Indeed, it was this close affinity with practical affairs which to some academic observers made the subjects of social ethics seem inappropriate in a university curriculum. Discussions of contemporary events, visitations by students to hospitals and asylums, and special studies of institutions or organizations, appeared to some critics a break with earlier traditions, and likely to obscure what Addison called 'the calm lights of mild philosophy.' Yet it was precisely this contact with social practitioners and this applicability of the case-system, which gave vitality to social ethics and have at last won for such studies general acceptance in academic life. These contacts of theory with practice involved a wide acquaintance, and often an affectionate intimacy, with the people who were actually doing things of which a lecturer was talking, and who saw with clear vision the ends which one was imperfectly trying to describe. English coöperators and French industrialists, German town-planners and American philanthropists, not only provided material for instruction, but in many instances became sustaining and inspiring friends.

It is difficult to single out from this large and cosmopolitan circle of acquaintance special instances of influence or leadership. A useful volume might be compiled of testimony concerning the writers and administrators who thus illustrate the modern social conscience. Such a survey would carry one all the way from the philosophy of Fichte to that of Felix Adler, and from the beginnings of the *Innere Mission* in Germany to the social settlements of Jane Addams and Robert Woods. For the present purpose, however, it is sufficient to recall three such friends, remote from each other in training and intention, but akin

It pays to follow one's best light — to put God and country first; ourselves afterward.

S. C. Armstrong

Samuel Chapman Armstrong

in social wisdom and spiritual insight. One was a gallant soldier, applying his militant spirit to the campaigns of peace; another was a joyous explorer both of nature and of life; and yet another was a scholar and statesman who was at the same time a mystic and seer. Each of these rare natures — '*Schöne Seelen*,' the Germans would call them — has a permanent place in the history of social service; yet each was also the teacher of a teacher, and intimacy with them remains a gracious memory which tempts one to repeat the thanksgiving of the Apostle Paul to 'the Father which hath made us meet to be partakers of the inheritance of the saints.'

The first of these enriching intimacies was that which I was permitted to maintain, through the last years of his life, with Samuel Chapman Armstrong of Hampton Institute. I had visited and inspected his school, and had reported to my students its dramatic history and its unprecedented methods; but it was a great surprise to me when, in 1890, General Armstrong appeared at my home in Cambridge and asked me to join his Board of Trustees. He died only three years later, leaving as his monument, not merely a great institution but a code of guiding principles and an example of inspiring leadership which have been wrought into a national tradition. Association with his work has brought me into intimate and confidential relations with some

181

of the wisest and most delightful of Americans, and has been for thirty-six years a labor of grateful love.

Few educational enterprises can boast so distinguished a list of trustees. Two presidents of the United States, several United States senators, with judges, clergymen, financiers, and educators, have generously and devotedly served the school. Was there ever better talk than in the late evenings, after the public meetings, by the friendly fireside of the principal, when Mr. Taft and Mr. Ogden and Bishop McVickar and President Low tossed the ball of conversation to and fro, while the rest of their fellow-members sat on the side-lines and cheered the game? Yet over all the deliberations of these busy men, who had snatched from their large affairs these intervals devoted to the care of the Negro race, there was always, whether during the administration of Armstrong's saintly successor, or of the not less consecrated chief now in command, a kind of *aura* in the memory of the Founder. Each decision was consciously directed to fulfil the General's desires or dreams. Behind the work of administrators and teachers still survives the undiminished force of the Armstrong tradition.

An institution may be built either on a plan or on a man. Sometimes a scheme is sketched on paper and endowed with money, but many an ample endowment has failed of its intention because the man has not been found. Sometimes, on the other hand, such a work begins with a man. He sees his vision and is obedient to it. He begins just where he is and with what he has, as though his dream said to him, 'Because I live ye shall live also.' Then the work develops as a living organism. It is not built; it grows. There will be all the routine and mechanism of an institution, but the machinery will respond to the human touch, as the whirling wheels of the factory convey the engine's power. The institution becomes the incarnation of a person. His word is made flesh. Thus it has been throughout the history of Hampton Institute. At each step we ask, 'What would the General say to this?' At each expansion of the work we say, 'How the General would rejoice in this!' The most precious asset of the school is the memory of its Founder.

In a word, General Armstrong was one of the small number of American citizens — perhaps a dozen, or even less — who must be without qualification described as great — great in work and great in character. He was noble in appearance, soldierly in bearing, fertile in plans, far-sighted in vision, unfailing in hope. In a degree hardly equalled in the history of education he had the gift of prophecy. He foresaw, and foretold with extraordinary precision, the tendencies and transitions which within the next twenty-five years were to revolutionize the principles of education. The training of the hand

and eye as well as of the mind — or rather, the training of the mind through observation and manual labor — the moral effect of technical skill, the conception of labor as a moral force, the test of education as efficiency, the subordination in industrial training of production to instruction, the advantages to both sexes of co-education in elementary schools, and the futility of education without discipline in thrift, self-help, love of work, and willingness to sacrifice — all these familiar maxims of modern vocational training were set forth with the confidence in which a creative genius instinctively anticipated the science of the future. Thus his career made an epoch, not only in the history of the Negro race, but in the theory of education; and his maxims and teachings have been accepted by alert and open minds, under the most varying conditions of race and place, in all parts of the civilized world. If it be consistent with Christian saintliness to be virile, daring, sanguine, brilliant, and sane; to work by faith when sight is denied; to communicate the contagion of a confident and sunny religious life, and to bear with joy the burden of a backward race, then the name of Samuel Armstrong is secure in its place among the saints of the modern world.

THE story of General Armstrong's life is a continuous and dramatic romance, which was well known by his contemporaries, but may be briefly recounted for

Samuel Chapman Armstrong

the sake of a generation which easily forgets.[1] He was born on Maui, one of the Hawaiian Islands, in 1839, the son of a missionary, to whom, with his devoted wife, had been committed the care of twenty-five thousand natives, and who became, not only their pastor, but their physician and the administrator of their industries; building sawmills as well as churches, performing surgical operations in the intervals of preaching the Gospel, and receiving a salary of four hundred dollars a year, with a fifty-dollar bonus for each child. In 1840 he was transferred to the principal church in Honolulu, and was soon appointed Minister of Public Instruction and a member of the native King's Privy Council. 'No other governmental officer,' the King said after his death, 'was brought into so close intimacy with the Government as a whole.' Meantime his wife, besides her carpentry, cooking, and prayers, added to the family income by bearing ten children, of whom Samuel was the sixth. He was a vigorous and venturesome boy, bred in a land of eternal summer and at home in its turquoise sea. When asked what he had chosen for his lifework, the boy answered that he was hesitating between the career of a missionary and that

[1] A more detailed narrative may be found in my *Education for Life*, Doubleday, Page & Co., 1918; written in connection with the Fiftieth Anniversary of the Foundation of Hampton Institute (chapters III and VIII), with a bibliography (pp. 329 ff.); and, more briefly, in my address, *Founders' Day at Hampton*, Houghton Mifflin Company, 1898.

of a pirate. Both of these social types were familiar
to him in Hawaii. In 1860 he was sent to Williams
College, and had the good fortune of living in the
home of the distinguished President, Mark Hopkins.
'Whatever good teaching I have done,' he later said,
'has been Mark Hopkins teaching through me.'

In 1861 the war broke out between the States,
and the young islander at first fancied himself a
neutral; but was soon seized by the war fever, and
reached the front just in time to be captured, with
his regiment, by Stonewall Jackson. Later, being
released from parole, he was at Gettysburg among
those who repelled Pickett's charge, and finally was
given command of a regiment of Negro troops, and
heard for the first time their 'spirituals' sung round
the camp-fire. 'One night I was drawn out of my
tent,' he said, 'by a wonderful chorus, "They look
like men of war,"' and this searching lyric, translating militarism into piety, became through later
life Armstrong's favorite hymn. After sharp fighting
in Virginia, he was disabled by fever, and missed
the attack on Richmond which his men were called
to make in his absence. They in their turn 'thanked
God that Captain Armstrong was not there, for if
he had been there, they would all have been either
in hell or in Richmond.'

At the end of the war, in April, 1865, Armstrong,
promoted to be a Brigadier-General of Volunteers,
was despatched to the Mexican border, where dis-

turbances threatened, and on the voyage, surrounded by his black soldiers, had a decisive spiritual experience. 'The night was warm,' he wrote, 'and many of us slept on deck, between the twin glories of sky and gulf, the splendor of sunset and the grandeur of the southern night.' His thoughts reverted to his boyhood's home and the Manual Labor School at Hilo, where dark-skinned boys were taught the elements of mechanic arts. Dreaming thus of his past, there came to him the vision of a similar school for the race he was now leading, and his Negro soldiers, lying on the deck below him, seemed to rise up and call for their redemption. Armstrong was no emotional enthusiast, but on the contrary a disciplined soldier; yet in this moment of exalted meditation his future stood plainly before him, and his life became from that point an act of obedience to the heavenly vision.

On his return from Mexico, the newly established Freedmen's Bureau seemed to offer a way for the realization of his dream, and he presented himself to General Howard, its experienced chief. Howard at first hesitated to yield to this youthful dreamer. 'Though already a general,' he wrote, 'Armstrong seemed to me very young. He spoke rapidly and wanted everything decided, if possible, on the spot.' It was a not unreasonable scepticism, for Armstrong, though he had been a regimental commander, was but twenty-seven years old. Finally it was arranged that he should be tested at what General Howard called 'the most delicate point in the Bureau,' and what Armstrong wrote was 'the hardest in the State.'

In the region round Hampton, Virginia, there were more than thirty thousand dependent and often starving 'contrabands.' Armstrong's immediate duty was to issue thousands of rations a day and relieve the necessities of these 'swarming camps'; but he soon recognized that these palliative measures were but temporary, and was led to recall his vision of a school which might fit a dependent race for an independent life. The American Missionary Association, a privately endowed organization of Congregationalists, endorsed the plan. General Howard made a modest appropriation of two thousand dollars; the 'Wood Farm' near Hampton, with its deserted mansion and mill, was approved as a site, and the young officer took temporary charge, 'in addition to present duty.' Thus, by an unanticipated migration across the ocean and the continent, and a not less dramatic transition in conviction and purpose, Armstrong reached the work which he was called to do. From Hawaii to New England, from indifference to the Negro race to the direction of its destiny, he had been led by influences which seemed fortuitous, but which pointed straight to the task for which all his training and experience had prepared the way. It was like the marvellous migration of the birds, controlled by an instinct more infallible than any conscious plan, and bearing them from the wintry North to the sunny South. So the migrating spirit of Armstrong bore him from war to peace, and from North to South, until at last he stood on the spot where his epoch-making work was to begin.

Hampton Institute, thus established as a by-product of Armstrong's life, soon became a commanding summons to him as a soldier. In 1868 he wrote to the American Missionary Association, 'I am too fully engaged here to be moved'; and by 1870 the new school was incorporated, and his destiny fixed. 'The thing to be done,' he wrote, 'is clear: to train selected Negro youths who shall go out and teach and lead their people, first by example, by getting land and homes; to give them not a dollar that they can earn for themselves; to teach respect for labor; to replace stupid drudgery with skilled hands; and in this way to build up an industrial system for the sake, not only of self-support and intelligent labor, but also for the sake of character.'

Armstrong's irresistible charm soon drew to him allies from the most competent and cultivated Northern homes. A daughter of the theologian, Leonard Bacon, directed the teaching; a daughter of what Armstrong called 'that splendid Woolsey family' taught the elements of industry to the girls; and a rugged, unassuming ex-soldier, Albert Howe, became farm manager. 'I promised,' Mr. Howe said fifty years later, 'to go until he could get some one else, but he never did, and I am here yet.' The motives and temper of this first circle of supporters are sufficiently indicated by a characteristic letter to one young friend :

HAMPTON, *September* 27, 1872

DEAR MISS LUDLOW :

Five millions of ex-slaves appeal to you. Will you come? Please telegraph if you can.

There's work here and brave souls are needed. If you care to sail into a good hearty battle, where there's no scratching and pin-sticking but great guns and heavy shot only used, come here. If you like to lend a hand where a good cause is shorthanded, come here.

We are growing rapidly; there is an inundation of students and we need more force. We want you as a teacher.

'Shall we whose souls are lighted?' etc. Please sing three verses before you decide, and then dip your pen in the rays of the morning light and say to this call, like the gallant old Col. Newcome, 'Adsum.'

Sincerely yours,

S. C. ARMSTRONG

The letter was like a bugle call, which Miss Ludlow obeyed as though summoned to action; and the band of loyal teachers of whom she was a representative, and whom Armstrong laughingly described as 'the noble army of martyrs' were in fact not consciously martyrs at all; but found in his exhilarating companionship an experience of privilege and joy.

The school thus modestly begun has had an expansion in endowment and diversified activity which would have astonished even the sanguine Armstrong. In 1868 it numbered one teacher, one matron, and fifteen pupils; in 1926 there were 129 teachers, 299 other paid assistants and employees, and 1017 students in regular classes, besides 1598 enrolments in the summer school, the extension classes, and the preparatory school. In the earliest printed statements, the receipts from 1867 to 1871 made a total of $138,769.80, of which only $7500 was for endowment; in 1926 the land, buildings, and equipment were valued at $2,316,184, and the invested funds exceeded $8,000,000.

Behind all this extraordinary development, and perpetuated by the loyal successors of the Founder, lie the maxims and principles which Armstrong's personality stamped upon the school. They were at first expressed in the most unstudied and casual forms, in talks to students or counsels to his staff, as a soldier might rally the courage of his men for attack, or steady them when threatened by reverse. 'For most people,' wrote one of his staff, 'an obstacle is something in the way, to stop going on, but for General Armstrong it merely meant something to climb over; and if he could not climb all the way over, he would go up as high as possible and then crow.' Armstrong himself taught the same lesson to his pupils in his parable of the woodchuck: 'Once there was a woodchuck. . . . Now woodchucks can't climb trees. Well, this woodchuck was chased by a dog and came to a tree. He knew that if he could get up this tree the dog could not catch him. Now woodchucks can't climb trees, but he had to, so he did!' His passionate intensity of temperament and desire is amusingly described in his precipitate form of correspondence: 'I have had a taste of blood; that is, I have had the taste of life and work, and cannot live without the arena. . . . Despair shakes his skinny hands and glares his hideous eyes on me to little purpose. I feel happy when all my powers of resistance are taxed.'

Gravity and humor, reflections and explosions, succeed each other both in his letters and in his talks to students; one never knew whether the next word would provoke smiles or tears. 'No recitation,' he once said, 'is complete without one good laugh.' 'Spend your life,' he taught his pupils, 'in doing what you can do well. If you can teach, teach. If you can't teach, but can cook well, do that. If a man can black boots better than anything else, what had he better do? Black boots? Yes. And if a girl can make an excellent nurse, and do that better than anything else, what had she better do? Nurse? Yes; she can do great good that way in taking care of the sick and suffering. Some of our girls have done great good

Samuel Chapman Armstrong

already in that way. Do what you can do well, and people will respect it and respect you. That is what the world wants of every one. It is a great thing in life to find out what you can do well. If a man can't do anything well, what's the matter with him? Lazy? Yes, that's it. A lazy man can't do anything well and no one wants him 'round. God didn't make the world for lazy people. . . . Go out from here to fight against sin. Fight the devil. Fight against evil and ignorance, disease, bad cooking. Help your people in teaching, in care of the sick, in improving land, in making better homes. Do what you can do well, and do it as well as you can. . . . Help your people by giving them what has been given you. Doing what can't be done is the glory of living.'

By degrees these improvised counsels took the form of fundamental teachings; and in his successive 'Reports' Armstrong announced with increasing lucidity the principles which have made his work an epoch in education. 'More and more,' he said in his 'Report of 1884,' 'I believe in labor as a moral force. While its pecuniary return to the student is important, and the acquired skill is equivalent to a working capital, the outcome of it in manly and womanly quality is, in the long run, perhaps the most valuable of all. The black man, like other men, finds it hard to see himself as he is seen. In the first excitement of freedom his true condition did not appear. He is kindly disposed, but lacks right intuitions or common sense. Wisdom will come to him, as it comes to all, through suffering and loss. He will learn more by his blunders than in any other way. Even the white man is not yet through his blundering period.'

And again : 'They are getting out of pupilage and are in the second and most difficult stage of progress. . . . Real progress is not in increase of wealth or power, but in gain in wisdom, in self-control, in guiding principles and in Christian ideas. That is the only true reconstruction ; to that Hampton's work is devoted. The future of the South is not to be as its past, and the Negro has no guarantee to his place within her borders unless he can make good his claim by showing himself to be an essential factor in her development. Back of any theory lies a personal experience, which forces us more and more strongly into faith in the as yet unmeasured power for good which a well-administered industrial system exerts over those who either by choice or by necessity are brought under its influence. Setting aside altogether what may be called its commercial value, we find it to be one of the strongest of moral forces that we have at our disposal, and are inclined to look upon it as the corner-stone of civilization for the two races with which we have to do.' 'In this, as in every country,' he said again, 'the future is safe and sure only as the educated and rich shall act out the

Samuel Chapman Armstrong

principles expressed in *Noblesse oblige*. There is no modern civilization for a leisure class; it is as dangerous as the lowest class. There is no elevation for those who do not work. . . . You will get what you work for — if for money, you are likely to get that; but do not complain if you do not get other good things that make home and country safer and better, unless you work for them. . . .'

Finally, through these hastily expressed but deeply felt convictions, he arrived at a working creed, which became summarized in the famous phrase, 'Education for life'; or in other words, the coöperation of the head, the hand, and the heart — the head to promote intelligence and insight, the hand to give facility and effectiveness, and the heart to reassure and fortify the conscience and will. These familiar maxims do not merely mean that the various functions of life deserve equal recognition, so that, as Booker Washington once said, 'There is as much dignity in tilling a field as in writing a poem.' They mean that, in addition to this balance of functions, the discipline of the parts reacts upon the welfare of the whole, and that the defect in either part diminishes education for life.

The education of the young had for the most part, under its early tradition among the whites, dealt with a fragment of life rather than with the whole. It had detached the training of the mind from the rest of experience. The three R's of the elementary school, the languages and histories of the academy, and the academic studies of the college, taken together, made one educated. And of course it was true that the instruction of the mind was an essential part of education. Yet such studies, after all, dealt with but a fraction of life. A boy might be equipped to enter college — and even to graduate from college — and yet remain in a large area of experience illiterate. He might not be able to see facts with his eyes, or shape them with his hands, or control them with his will. At this point entered the deeper significance of industrial education. It might, of course, be justified by its economic value. A good hand-worker can make a better living to-day than the average clerk or minister. Much more fundamental, however, is the effect of industrial training upon character, and its product in precision, thoroughness, and intellectual integrity.

Here was the great pedagogical discovery of that era — that the habit of mind promoted by the work of the hands has its part in the training of the mind and will, and that industrial education must be included in any comprehensive scheme of education for life. The three ways of education coöperate with each other to make a whole life. Manual work needs mental training to make it efficient, and at the same time gives to head-work accuracy, precision, honesty, and skill; and, still further, the consecration of the heart gives both to head and hand their devotion, patience, and unselfishness. In other words, the new education takes the whole of life for its problem : the eyes to see, the hands to shape, the body to be the servant of the will, the will directing and restraining both the body and the mind. It repeats the great word spoken by the ancient Greek philosopher, 'It is necessary for a man to be whole.'

Such were the maxims of the new education which Armstrong reiterated and enforced throughout his career. Thus as early as 1872 he wrote : 'The moral advantages of industrial training over all other methods justify the expense'; and again in 1888, 'Experience has strengthened my conviction of labor as a moral force'; and yet again in 1891, 'Character is the best outcome of the labor system'; and in 1892, 'Honestly giving value for value, labor becomes a stepping stone, a ladder, to education, to all higher things, to success, manhood, and character.' In other words, industrial education not only increases wage-earning capacity, but promotes fidelity, accuracy, honesty, persistency, and intelligence. The capacity to make a living becomes enlarged into the capacity to make a life.

The busy scene, therefore, which meets one at Hampton, of cooking and carpentering, of blacksmithing and agriculture, should be regarded, not merely as a preparation for bread-winning, but as the outward expression of that spiritual enterprise which Hampton fundamentally represents — the way to trustworthy manhood and self-respecting womanhood. The training of the hand is at the same time a clarifying of the mind and a purifying of the heart. The classroom, the trade-school, the farm, and the church, are coördinated agents of education as it is conceived at Hampton. Education and religion meet in this attempt to deal with the whole of life. Holiness is but another name for wholeness. No life is whole that is not holy, and no life is holy that is not whole. That is the daily confession, in worship and in work, of Hampton's educational creed.

In all parts of the world — in India, in Greece, in Southern Africa, this 'Hampton idea' has been welcomed and imitated, and the pedagogical genius of Armstrong has made him the recognized prophet of education for life. Indeed, it is one of the most dramatic ironies in the history of education that this conception of the pupil as an integral unit — so that, as a great English teacher has lately said, 'Strictly speaking there is no such thing as a dull boy' — and this resolution to coördinate diverse faculties as members one of another, should have been first clearly conceived and practically illustrated, not in a conspicuous institution for the dominant race, but in the unobserved administration of a school for negroes; and that the guiding principles of modern education may be traced, as an original discovery, to the modest work for a backward race developed by the untaught insight of the founder of Hampton Institute.

Yet it would be a most incomplete record of Armstrong's career to set him among educational experts and remember him as a great teacher only. The secret of his influence — indeed, the qualities which made him a great teacher — were the product of the extraordinary union of confidence and consecration, of light-heartedness and high-mindedness, which marked his character. He was the most undiscouraged and joyous of reformers. 'I never gave up anything,' he said at the end of his life, 'or sacrificed anything in my life.' His attitude toward both teachers and students under his charge was that of a companion, almost of a playmate, as though he were repeating the great words reported of Jesus Christ in his last hours: 'These things have I spoken unto you, that my joy might remain in you, and that your joy might be full.' Yet within this gay demeanor, which sent teachers and pupils singing on their way, was a stability of religious faith which sustained his entire experience. Religion to him was not the reservation of a part of life, but the education of the whole of it. 'If any man will do his will, he shall know of the doctrine.' His creed was short, 'the shorter the better,' he said — '"Simply to thy cross I cling," is enough for me.' There was in him a complete naturalness in the Christian life, a simplicity which was in Christ; or, as the passage may be more accurately translated, 'a straightforwardness which is toward Christ.' In a word, he had taken over into the work of a missionary the habits of a soldier. He was fighting a good fight; he could endure hardness as a good soldier of Jesus Christ; he was unentangled by the affairs of this world, that he might please him who had chosen him to be a soldier. Nothing could defeat or depress such a commander; no occasion was so discouraging as to suggest surrender.

As I recall the incidents which testify to this emancipation from circumstance there comes to mind one scene in the course of his mendicant journeys to the North. It was at a little suburban church, far down a side street, on a winter night, in the midst of a driving storm of sleet. There was, as nearly as possible, no congregation present; a score or so of humble people, showing no sign of any means to contribute, scattered through the empty spaces, and a dozen restless boys kicking their heels in the front pew. Then, before this emptiness and hopelessness rose the worn, gaunt soldier, as bravely and gladly as if a multitude were hanging upon his words; and his deep-sunk eyes looked out beyond the bleakness of the scene into the world of his ideals, and the cold little place was aglow with the fire that was in him, until it was like the scene on the Mount that was not any less wonderful and glistening because only three undiscerning followers were per-

mitted to see the glory. It was, as Browning wrote
when he 'flung out of the little chapel' where he had
taken refuge from the rain and found the Lord Christ
revealed :

> 'So He said, and so it befalls.
> God who registers the cup
> Of mere cold water, for His sake
> To a disciple rendered up,
> Disdains not His own thirst to slake
> At the poorest love was ever offered ;
> And because it was my heart I proffered,
> With true love trembling at the brim,
> He suffers me to follow Him.'

It was inevitable that a life thus lived must be
soon exhausted, as though it verified the Psalmist's
saying, 'The zeal of thine house hath eaten me up.'
On Thanksgiving Day, 1891, Armstrong, then but
fifty-two years old, was speaking in a small town
near Boston, when he suddenly faltered and sank
into the arms of one of his black pupils. He survived
for two years, with a broken body but an unbroken
will, and died suddenly on May 11, 1893. His body
was laid, as he had desired, among those of his students who had died at the school, 'where one
of them,' as he directed, 'would have been put had
he died next' ; and devoted friends made of his grave
a symbol of his life. At its head was set a huge fragment of volcanic rock, laboriously brought from his
island home in the Pacific, and at its foot a quartz
boulder hewn from the Berkshire Hills, where he

had been trained. The monument speaks of the character it commemorates, volcanic in temperament, granitic in persistency; with energy like a mountain on fire but with steadiness and stability as of one who had lifted up his eyes to the hills and found help.

With Armstrong's will was found, after his death, a paper of memoranda, containing a last message to his fellow-workers and family. His work as an educator was no longer his chief concern, and his final reflections turned to the deeper sources of his confidence and strength. The administrator, the reformer, the soldier, had become the humble and prayerful saint.

MEMORANDA

Now when all is bright, the family together, and there is nothing to alarm, and very much to be thankful for, it is well to look ahead, and perhaps to say the things that I should wish known should I suddenly die :

I wish to be buried in the school graveyard among the students, where one of them would have been put had he died next.

I wish no monument or fuss whatever over my grave ; only a simple headstone, no text or sentiment inscribed, only my name and date. I wish the simplest funeral service without sermon or attempt at oratory — a soldier's funeral.

ARMSTRONG'S GRAVE

Samuel Chapman Armstrong

I hope there will be enough friends to see that the work of the school shall continue. Unless some shall make sacrifices for it, it cannot go on.

A work that requires no sacrifice does not count for much in fulfilling God's plans. But what is commonly called sacrifice is the best, happiest use of one's self and one's resources — the best investment of time, strength, and means. He who makes no such sacrifice is most to be pitied. He is a heathen because he knows nothing of God.

In the school the great thing is not to quarrel; to pull all together; to refrain from hasty, unwise words and actions; to unselfishly and wisely seek the best good of all; and to get rid of workers whose temperaments are unfortunate — whose heads are not level; no matter how much knowledge or culture they may have. Cantankerousness is worse than heterodoxy.

I wish no effort at a biography of myself made. Good friends might get up a pretty good story, but it would not be the whole truth. The truth of a life usually lies deep down — we hardly know ourselves — God only does. I trust his mercy. The shorter one's creed the better. 'Simply to thy cross I cling' is enough for me.

I am most thankful for my parents, my Hawaiian home, for war experiences, and college days at Williams, and for life and work at Hampton. Hampton has blessed me in so many ways; along with it have come the choicest people of the country for my friends and helpers, and then such a grand chance to do something directly for those set free by the war, and indirectly for those who were conquered; and Indian work has been another great privilege.

Few men have had the chance that I have had. I never gave up or sacrificed anything in my life — have been, seemingly, guided in everything.

Prayer is the greatest power in the world. It keeps us near to God. My own prayer has been most weak, wavering, inconstant, yet has been the best thing I have ever done. I think this is a universal truth — what comfort is there in any but the broadest truths?

I am most curious to get a glimpse of the next world. How will it all seem? Perfectly fair, perfectly natural, no doubt. We ought not to fear death. It is friendly.

The only pain that comes at the thought of it is for my true faithful wife and blessed dear children. But they will be brave about it all, and in the end stronger. They are my greatest comfort.

Hampton must not go down. See to it, you who are true to the black and red children of the land, and to just ideas of education.

The loyalty of my old soldiers and of my students has been an unspeakable comfort.

It pays to follow one's best light — to put **God** and country first; ourselves afterwards.

Taps has just sounded.

S. C. ARMSTRONG

CHAPTER X

HENRY DRUMMOND

A SECOND friendship which enriched the experiences and widened the horizon of academic life was that which I was permitted to hold with Henry Drummond of Glasgow.

Never was one saint more different in type from another than Drummond was from Armstrong. The rugged soldier, who directed his school as if it were a regiment, was abrupt and explosive in manner, eloquent only by force, a virile, impetuous, impassioned saint. Drummond, on the other hand, was a gracious, refined, almost dainty, gentleman ; bred in luxury, restrained in speech, and accomplishing by charm what Armstrong won by compulsion. Of Armstrong it might be said, 'He taught them as one having authority'; of Drummond it might be said, 'They wondered at the gracious words which proceeded out of his mouth.' Armstrong was a Moses, leading an enslaved people out of captivity into the opportunities and perils of liberty ; Drummond, like Paul, was converted from a scholar into a missionary, and applied his learning and life to 'preach the gospel of peace and bring glad tidings of good things.' Yet these diverse characters had the same lesson to teach, of a faith which was known by its works and a love which was the greatest thing in the world. Companionship with these masters was a spiritual education.

Acquaintance with Henry Drummond was, on the whole, the most exhilarating incident of my academic life. When, in 1887, I learned that he had yielded to Mr. Moody's urgent invitation, and was to visit this country in the interest of the Northfield School, I wrote to claim him for the Harvard Chapel, and in October, after a summer of arduous service in the United States and Canada, he reached Cambridge, and during a week of intense activity was a delightful guest in my home.

It was a pleasant surprise, many years later, to find in the biography of Drummond a letter, written by him to his father in Scotland, in which he generously describes this visit. 'Harvard College,' he writes, ' (the college of Lowell, Emerson, Longfellow, Fiske, etc.) is *the* college of the country, and under Unitarian auspices ; so that I was told it would be impossible to do anything there ; but the work was really better than anywhere. I lived with one of the Professors, a Unitarian, but I found no difference between him and myself, and I never saw a more lovely Christian home.' Throughout this busy week his conversation was in the highest degree vivacious and contagious, as of an unspoiled and unconventional man of the world ; and the profound impression he made upon our students was in no small part the effect of an unprofessional manner and an unaffected simplicity.

Henry Drummond

In 1890, I had the privilege of spending a week-end with him at Glasgow; inspected with him on Saturday night the sad scenes of excess in squalid streets, and listened with him on Sunday to the preaching of Marcus Dods — 'the greatest influence in many directions,' Drummond said of him, 'that ever came across my life.' During these days of happy companionship I was permitted in prolonged conversation by day and night to catch glimpses of Drummond's elusive but transparent soul. It would be a presumption to speak of intimacy with him, for he spoke little of himself or his work, but with the most engaging candor of events and teachers and preachers and books and sport. The range of his interests and studies and explorations could be discovered through the disguise of this casual talk. 'There comes a time in the Spring,' he said, 'when a Scotchman must fish or burst'; and as I fingered his bookshelves and inquired what writer had lately appealed to him, it was a surprise to have him answer, 'Mazzini.'

On his second visit to America, in 1893, when he gave at the Lowell Institute his lectures on 'The Ascent of Man,' he found it more prudent to hide in a hotel during the tardy revision of his work; but used my home as a place of departure for a series of talks to Harvard students, reporting to me, among many entertaining observations of the American character, the friendly counsel of his stenographer in the Boston hotel concerning the brand of chewing-

gum which she commended for his use. In the intervals between these lectures he spoke repeatedly to
our young men, with a persuasiveness which was
wholly captivating, and which made religion not
only a real but a joyous experience. 'Above all
things,' he said to them, 'do not touch Christianity
unless you are willing to put the kingdom of God
first. I promise you a miserable existence if you put
it second.'

These three brief opportunities of domestic companionship leave an indelible and almost unique
impression of physical and spiritual charm. So har-
monious a nature, one so completely free from artifi-
ciality or excess, so Greek in symmetry and so
Christian in consecration, has rarely been called to
interpret the complexity and confusion of modern
life. The effect of his brief visitations, through public
talks and private conferences, constituted a genuine
revival of religion, and justified the faith of the
Preachers to the University in the responsiveness
of youth to a genuine and masculine appeal. An
estimate of Drummond by his lifelong friend John
Watson (Ian Maclaren) might seem an extravagant
utterance of admiration, but it would be accepted
by great numbers of listeners as a sober conclusion
reached under the spell of a beautiful soul : 'After a
lifetime's intimacy, I do not remember my friend's
failing. Without pride, without envy, without selfish-
ness, without vanity, moved only by goodwill and

Henry Drummond

spiritual ambitions, responsive ever to the touch of God and every noble impulse, faithful, fearless, magnanimous, Henry Drummond was the most perfect Christian I have known or expect to see this side of the grave.'

HENRY DRUMMOND was born at Glasgow in 1851, the second son of a properous and serious-minded merchant.[1] He was reared in refinement and luxury, and made his home throughout his life in a spacious house next to that in which he was born, on the 'Circus' above the 'West End Park' of Glasgow. As a boy he did not fit easily into the standardized methods of Scotch education, but was passionately fond of reading and of science, dabbling in what were then called electro-biology and mesmerism, alert at games and distinguished at fishing and skating; in a word, the charming son of a prosperous home. He grew into an erect and agile manhood to which would at once be applied the word distinction. Scrupulous, even fashionable, in attire, with a swinging gait and a care-free manner, he gave the general impression, not of a scholar or saint, but of a cultivated and captivating man of the world. He never married, and, though ordained to the ministry,

[1] The story is admirably told in the masterly volume of Sir George Adam Smith, *The Life of Henry Drummond*, 1898; and in the *Memorial Sketch*, by W. Robertson Nicoll and John Watson (Ian Maclaren), prefixed to the collection of Drummond's addresses and sermons under the title, *The Ideal Life and other Unpublished Addresses*, 1899.

never presented himself as a parson, but rather as an urbane gentleman to whom religion was almost a form of sport. The name he went by among younger men, his biographer reports, was 'The Prince,' and there was an aspect of nobility and graciousness about him that justified the title. What at once arrested attention as one met him was the extraordinary and commanding penetration of his eyes. It was not that he fixed one by his gaze, but that his complete and unwavering interest in the person before him gave an irresistible impression of insight and discernment. The natives in Central Africa, it is said, called him by a name which signifies 'He who looks' or 'gazes,' 'whether because of his careful scrutiny of minerals, insects, etc., or because of the keenness of his eyes when he looked into another man's face, is unknown.' It was not a physical brilliancy, but a spiritual radiance, which illuminated, comprehended, and inspirited, and it became a powerful though unconscious instrument of Drummond's persuasion and appeal. 'It was,' Ian Maclaren says, 'as Plato imagined it would be in the Judgment: one soul was in contact with another — nothing between. No man could be double or base or mean or impure before that eye.'

With this equipment, of a refinement approaching elegance and a scientific habit of mind singularly remote from the studies encouraged among his fellows, Drummond in 1866 entered the University of

Henry Drummond

Edinburgh, attaining there such moderate success in the 'Arts Course' that he failed to receive his degree, and later described himself as a 'two thirds M.A.' In fact, his nomadic mind had already ventured into literary wanderings which his accredited teachers regarded as dissipating or dangerous. The first of these passions was for Ruskin, then at the height of his powers, holding high his 'Lamp of Sacrifice' and preaching his gospel of a social order which should be open 'Unto this Last.' Next to Ruskin, as Professor Nicoll testifies, Drummond put Emerson, whose searching aphorisms powerfully affected Drummond's teaching and style. To these rash adventures of the spirit was added the influence of William Ellery Channing and Frederick Robertson, between whom, as Nicoll suggestively adds, 'the parallels have never been properly drawn out.' Thus, in the most susceptible years of Drummond's student life, both his style and his thought were moulded by these uncanonical prophets, who may have contributed more than he realized to that sanity and lucidity of expression which were soon to be such effective instruments.

From the University Drummond passed, in conformity with his father's desire, to the Divinity College of the Free Church; but there, although dutifully accepting instruction in Hebrew and Apologetics, his real concern was to find a way through natural science to a science of faith; and while yet a student he wrote an essay on the 'Doctrine of Creation,' commenting on the 'Origin of Species' in language which though immature was suggestive of his later work. One can well understand why his teachers felt some concern for a student who insisted on adding to his studies in divinity attendance at scientific lectures in the University, and whose reading was of Ruskin, Carlyle, and 'much poetry,' rather than of Calvinism and the composition of the Pentateuch. In fact, the authorities of the University saw in the young theological student the making of a man of science, and in 1872 offered him a tutorship in geology.

The emancipation from ecclesiastical provincialism became complete when Drummond, in 1873, migrated to Germany for a semester at Tübingen — a visit which made its mark on his whole life through the acquisition of broader sympathy and tolerance. He returned from Germany, still bent on applying the method of science to the problems of religion, and in an essay read to a society of fellow-students on 'Spiritual Diagnosis' he anticipated much of the procedure now so universally commended in education, and known as the case-system. 'The medical student,' he said, 'in the clinic has much to teach to the student of theology; for he approaches each case for its own sake and subordinates generalities to personal examination. It should be the same with religion. The minister is a physician of the soul, and his primary task is that of spiritual diagnosis.'

Henry Drummond

It was a youthful and undeveloped paper, but it was in effect a striking premonition of the notable teaching proposed in 1926 by the distinguished American clinician Dr. Richard Cabot, under the title 'A Clinical Year for Theological Students.'

At this point in the undetermined course of Drummond's life occurred the dramatic event which in one abrupt transition gave a new direction and momentum to his career. In the summer of 1873, the two American evangelists, Moody and Sankey, arrived unheralded in England, and began a series of popular meetings which appeared to many observers too crude and aggressive to be acceptable in Great Britain. Mr. Moody was a short, thickset, burly man, whom a casual observer would be likely to place, where in fact he had once made his living, as a dealer in leather. He had the manner of a successful 'drummer,' and the present generation might describe his method as 'selling religion.' On the other hand, he immediately impressed all hearers as completely single-minded and sincere, and his addresses, like those of Abraham Lincoln, were packed with anecdote, reminiscence, wit, and genuine feeling. He was genuinely conscious of his own limitations; and while once a guest in my home, with his wife, for a week of meetings with Harvard students, inquired one morning about the duties of a professor. Being told that one usually lectured four or five times a week during the whole winter, he said across the table to his wife, 'Emma, this is no place for us. I only last three weeks.' He was not, in his own opinion, as successful at Harvard University as in many other colleges, but he felt sure that this was his own fault rather than ours. In other words, his prodigious popularity had not cost him his simplicity or humility. He remained a plain man, who knew himself to be about his Father's business.

Such was the revivalist who was soon stirring great multitudes in England and Scotland by his virile and searching appeal. Nothing could have seemed more improbable than that his message should have touched the refined — not to say fastidious — nature of a youth like Henry Drummond, whose enthusiasm was dedicated to science and literature, and who had but languid concern for theology. He might wish well to these crude Americans, but his tastes, his training, and his sense of humor seemed likely to make these familiar talks and this trivial music appear unalluring or even repulsive. Then occurred a spiritual transition which can be compared with nothing less than the experience of the Apostle Paul. Behind the extraordinary power of popular appeal which Mr. Moody possessed, he had maintained two principles of his work which were inconspicuous but fundamental. The first was derived from his observation that the emotional excitement of the crowd must be steadied and reënforced by the specialist's care of the individual.

Henry Drummond

His converts must be followed, sustained, confirmed. There must be a clinic as well as a lecture, a case-method, like that which Drummond had suggested in his 'Spiritual Diagnosis.' Moody's after-meetings were to his mind the core of his work. The second principle he had reached was derived from his own sense of limitation. His hope for the future of religion was set on the discovery of young men who should be intellectually as well as piously fit to direct these clinics of the soul. The first principle, of individual conference, drew Drummond to Moody; the second principle, of selected diagnosticians, led Moody to see in Drummond a providential instrument; and the academic student, with all his sensitive and restrained habits, his love of Ruskin and Emerson, threw himself with a complete and untiring devotion into the work of an itinerant evangelist.

It was not a catastrophic revelation, such as blinded young Saul near Damascus, but it was not less a literal conversion — a turning round — of the course of Drummond's life; so that he became, not, as he might have anticipated, a teacher of geology or physics, but a missionary of Christ to liberally educated young men, as though he repeated in his new vocation the pledge of the Apostle, 'I live; yet not I, but Christ liveth in me.' Neither the homely and unpolished manner of the American exhorter, nor the tasteless melodies of his zealous colleague, disguised from their young disciple the sincerity and insight of their message. God, he felt sure, had chosen the foolish things of the world to confound the wise, and things which are despised to bring to naught things that are. Drummond gave his whole heart to the 'Great Mission,' and soon, by his gracious charm and his intimate understanding of university students, became the chief interpreter in Great Britain of Moody's message. Young men could not resist his winning candor and his searching eye. 'It was the way Mr. Drummond laid his hand on my shoulder,' said one youth, 'and looked me in the face, that led me to Christ.' 'I do not believe,' Drummond wrote, 'there has ever been such an opportunity for work in the history of the Church. . . . I feel I must go forward. The pointing of the Finger has grown plainer and more unmistakable.'

This singular intimacy of the rugged evangelist and the sensitive young scholar — Drummond was but twenty-three years old — survived with unbroken confidence on both sides throughout Mr. Moody's life; and when Drummond was about to sail from America after his second journey, and had a few days in Boston, with invitations to dine with Longfellow and Holmes, the news came to him, he writes, that 'eight hundred miles off, away by Lake Erie, were two men who were more to me than philosopher or poet, and it only required a moment's thought to convince me that for me at least a visit to America would be much more than incomplete without a visit to Mr. Moody and Mr. Sankey. It was hard, I must say, to give up Longfellow, but I am one of those who think that the world is not dying for poets so much as for preachers. I set off at once'; and, as his biographer reports, 'burst in, uninvited and unannounced, upon the astonished evangelists at Cleveland.' The mission of Moody was to the masses of plain people, who welcomed the unlettered ways of the evangelist and the sentimentalism of his companion's singing; the mission of Drummond was to the universities, where he spoke the language and had the manner of academic intimacy.

From these meetings in the Scotch universities he was called to the still more difficult task of making religion real to the social aristocracy of London, and with much reluctance, but with extraordinary simplicity and naturalness, he addressed assemblages at Grosvenor House, the London home of the Duke of Westminster. Here gathered statesmen, publicists, authors, and ladies of fashion, and heard, to their surprise, not a discussion of evolution by the author of 'Natural Law,' but an unadorned and convincing talk on personal religion, ending with spontaneous and unstudied prayer. Some critics were inclined to scoff at this importation of revivalism into fashionable life, and wrote of the 'canny author of "Natural Law," who has an eye to dramatic effect far more

acute than is possessed by most professional drama-
tists or actors. . . . To be able to collect, even under
a ducal roof, four or five hundred people, many of
them of the highest distinction, social and intellectual, is a triumph of ingenuity.' The fact was, however, that these listeners at Grosvenor House turned
out to be of the same human stuff with the crowds
which hung on Mr. Moody's words, conscious of
their spiritual emptiness, eager for the restoration
of faith and hope, but needing for their guidance
the voice of a scholar and the manner of a cultivated
gentleman. 'Sooner or later,' Drummond later said
of the intellectual life in its relation to religion, 'the
conquest comes; sooner or later, whether it be art
or music, history or philosophy, Christianity utilizes
the best that the world finds, and gives it a niche
in the temple of God.' [1]

The next phases of Drummond's life were hardly
less surprising than this evangelism; for he soon
became, again with dramatic likeness to the experience of Saint Paul — first a great traveller, and
then a writer who gave to the Christian religion fresh
reality and significance. In 1877, he was appointed
a lecturer on natural science in the Free Church
College of Glasgow; an institution which, it is said,
had been founded to defend religion from the threat-

---

[1] The evangelistic work of Drummond is faithfully described by
Cuthbert Lennox, in his volume, *The Practical Life-Work of Henry
Drummond*, 1901, with a bibliography of writings, pp. 225 ff.

ening invasion of the doctrine of evolution, but which gave Drummond an opportunity to affirm the analogies of science and faith, and to prepare his book on 'Natural Law in the Spiritual World.' According to the beneficent schedule of British universities more than half of each year is unencumbered by lecturing, and Drummond used his ample holidays, first in 1879 by joining an expedition of Professor Geikie's on a geological survey among the American Rockies; and then in 1883 by a more venturesome expedition to East Central Africa, where he found almost equal delight among missionaries, wonders of nature, and encounters with great game. The story of this half-year is modestly and graphically told by him in his 'Tropical Africa,' in which, as he says, he describes the country, not primarily as one to be explored, but as 'one to be pitied and redeemed.' The book is an unpretentious record of lonely wanderings, with observations of slave-traders and lions and white ants, but is primarily concerned with the heroism and sacrifices of the Scotch missionaries, to visit whom was his special mission. Still another journey, to the New Hebrides, was added to these Pauline wanderings; and here again nature and religion joined in their appeal. The birds and banyan trees, the volcanoes and earthquakes, on the one hand, and the cannibals and missionaries on the other, gave him exhilaration and delight. 'I do not think,' he wrote, 'I ever had such an interesting tour in my life. I was in Mr. Paton's tanna and saw all his painted cannibals. But for the missionary with me, I should now be — inside them!'

Then occurred another dramatic incident in this diversified career. Drummond had left his 'Natural Law in the Spiritual World' to be published after his departure for Africa in January, and he received no news from England until November. Then, one night, in the heart of Africa, a package of letters reached him, and he found himself famous. His book had taken Great Britain and America by storm; had reached a series of editions, and had been reviewed with every shade of appreciation and opposition. The 'Spectator' had said of it: 'No book of our time (with the exception of Dr. Mozley's University Sermons) has shown such a power of stating the moral and practical truths of religion so as to make them take fresh hold of the mind and vividly impress the imagination.' On the other hand, many theologians found it unevangelical and many scientific critics found it unscientific; and Drummond was attacked, not without bitterness, from both sides, as heretical in religion and as ill-informed in science. He had maintained the thesis that the laws of nature run up into the spiritual sphere; that one could 'reconstruct a spiritual religion on the lines of nature'; and his application of this thesis in chapters on biogenesis degeneration, parasitism, and other terms of science, was in the highest degree novel and fascinating.

It may be seriously questioned whether so complete an identity can be safely affirmed, and whether Drummond was not in fact pointing out striking analogies and suggestive affinities, rather than 'natural laws continuing through the universe of spirit.' No less an authority than Huxley had reached precisely the opposite conclusion and found in the defiance of the law of evolution, and in the revival of the unfit rather than the survival of the fit, the distinguishing mark of human life. Drummond's warm friend John Watson goes so far as to intimate that Drummond 'lost all interest in "Natural Law" . . . and would have been quite willing to see it withdrawn from the public.' Yet it remains an extraordinary fact that by its lucid and persuasive style and its spiritual insight the book made religion real to thousands of people who had fancied it an artificial or superadded possession. It was, as Dr. Watson says, 'the idyll of religion,' or as one Anglican critic described it, 'the best book he had ever read upon Christian experience.'

A different estimate may be reasonably reached concerning his second book, 'The Ascent of Man,' which made the material of his Lowell Lectures at Boston in 1893, where the addresses were welcomed by such a throng of hearers that their repetition was demanded. Here was offered an argument which was in some degree corrective of the former volume. Instead of the laws of nature running up into spiritual life, there were now described the laws of spiritual life as foreshadowed in the cruder processes of nature. Evolution must take account, not merely of man as a part of the animal creation, but of the whole man and 'the great moral facts.' 'The moral and religious forces must no more be left out than the forces of gravitation or life.' To the struggle for life must be added the struggle for the life of others. Nutrition and reproduction in the animal world become altruism in the moral world. Self-regarding functions evolve into other-regarding functions. The rudimentary processes of nature are prophetic of the ascent of man. 'As the one struggle waxes the other wanes.' 'The path of progress and the path of altruism are one.'

Here was unquestionably a sublime theme nobly treated and copiously illustrated. The successive chapters, on the evolution of body, mind, language, and parenthood, are beyond doubt a permanent contribution to evolutionary ethics; and the chapter on the 'Evolution of a Mother' deserves to be set beside the doctrine which John Fiske regarded as his most original discovery, the far-reaching consequence of the prolongation of human infancy. All these qualities make the volume, as John Watson has said, 'the poem of evolution,' 'a fascinating combination of scientific detail and spiritual imagination.'

Henry Drummond

Yet it must be admitted that these volumes, suggestive and brilliant as they were, are not the writings of Drummond which have retained most vitality. In his case, as in that of many authors, the central task with which he was profoundly concerned threw off in its course casual, and, as the author thought, ephemeral by-products, which had in them the spark of genius and lit a flame of appreciation. Wide as was the acceptance of the 'Ascent of Man' as an assuring and mediating gospel, it did not compare with the popular enthusiasm for his short addresses on 'The Progress of Christianity' and 'The Changed Life'; still less with his masterpiece of lyric utterance, 'The Greatest Thing in the World,' which was soon reproduced in countless forms, and had, as I can testify from personal observation, the unusual distinction among religious essays of being hawked at the street-corners of Boston by enterprising newsboys.

Finally, among these varied explorations of nature and life, must be recalled the contagious gaiety with which during the last years of his short life Henry Drummond gave himself to the study of those complex creatures called Boys. Drummond had, as his biographer says, 'the secret of being a boy without leaving his manhood behind.' Childless himself, he saw, as did his childless Master, the Kingdom of Heaven in the spirit of little children. Standardized Sunday Schools repelled him by their artificial constraints; but a real boy, even a ragamuffin, stirred his own sunny boyishness into sympathetic radiance. It happened that in 1889 a Glasgow merchant had hit on a plan of resuscitating a Sunday School by enlisting the boys in a company for drill, and out of this modest enterprise grew the great movement of the Boys' Brigade, 'to promote among boys the habits of obedience, reverence, discipline, self-respect, and all that tends toward a true Christian manliness.' Into this school of masculine piety, Drummond threw himself with prodigious enthusiasm, drilling, advising, writing, as though he had found the key of morals in the discipline of play. Talking in my own home one day of this new and engrossing association, he said: 'You can take the most restless boy in town, put a five-penny cap on his head and a six-penny belt round his waist, and say in a loud voice "tenshun," and he will stand stock still until you tell him to move.'

The same words occur in a detailed description of the Brigade which Drummond gave to the students of Harvard University, and which by a fortunate accident was fully reported. 'The idea of the Brigade,' Drummond said, 'is this: It is a new movement for turning out boys, instead of savages. The average boy, as you know, is a pure animal. He is not evolved; and, unless he is taken in hand by somebody who cares for him and who understands him, he will be very apt to make a mess of his life — not to speak of the lives of other people. We endeavor to get hold of this animal. You do not have the article here, and do not quite understand the boy I mean. The large cities of the Old World are infested by hundreds and thousands of these ragamuffins, as we call them — young roughs who have nobody to look after them. The Sunday School cannot handle these boys. The old method was for somebody to form them into a class and try to get even attention from them. Half the time was spent in securing order. The new method is simply this : You get a dozen boys together and, instead of forming them into a class, you get them into some little hall, and put upon every boy's head a little military cap that costs in our country something like twenty cents, and you put round his waist a belt that costs about the same sum, and you call him a soldier. You tell him : "Now, Private Hopkins, stand up. Hold up your head. Put your feet together." And you can order that boy about till he is black in the face, just because he has a cap on his head and a belt around his waist. The week before you could do nothing with him. If he likes it, you are coming next Thursday night. He is not doing any favor by coming. You are doing him a favor by coming ; and if he does not turn up at eight o'clock, to the second, the door will be locked. If his hair is not brushed and his face washed, he cannot enter. Military discipline is established from the first moment. You give the boys three fourths of an hour's drill again, and in a short time you have introduced quite a number of virtues into that boy's character. You have taught him instant obedience. If he is not obedient, you put him into the guard-house, or tell him he will be drummed out of the regiment; and he will never again disobey. If he is punctual and does his drill thoroughly, tell him that at the end of the year he will get a stripe. He will get a cent's worth of braid. You have his obedience, punctuality, intelligence, and attention for a year for one cent. Then you have taught him courtesy. He salutes you, and feels a head taller. Everything is done as if you were a real captain and he a real private. He calls you "Captain." Each boy has a rifle that costs a dollar; but there is no firing. There is a bayonet drill without a bayonet. The first year they have military drill, and the second year bayonet exercises — an absolute copy of the army drill. The Brigade inculcates a martial, but not a warlike, spirit. The only inducement to bring the boys together at first is the drill. You might think it is a very poor one, but it is about the strongest inducement you could offer. That is the outward machinery; but it is a mere take-in. The boy doesn't know it. The real object of the Brigade is to win that boy for Christianity — to put it quite plainly. It does not make the slightest secret of its aim.'

Henry Drummond

Summer camps, ambulance classes, working boys' clubs — all grew out of this transformation of Sunday Schools, which, in Drummond's belief, did not teach the art of war or 'foster the war spirit,' but 'employed military organization, drill, and discipline as the most stimulating and interesting means of securing the attention of a volatile class and of promoting self-respect, courtesy, *esprit de corps*, and a host of kindred virtues.'

Such was the last expression of Drummond's joyous delight in life. In 1894, a subtle and malignant affection of the bones attacked him, and after three years of intense suffering, relieved by an unfailing faith, and brightened by flashes of playfulness and charm, he died, in March, 1897, when but forty-six years of age.

No brief summary of Drummond's extraordinary influence could be more suggestive than the story of his work in 1893 at Harvard University. He spoke on one Sunday evening in the University Chapel, not as a preacher, but as a college man to his associates ; he held a series of meetings in the following week which were attended by throngs of eager youths ; and this brief ministry left behind it a wave of religious response, which broadened like the wake of a departing steamship until it spread into every corner and social set of college life. His method was that of Mr. Moody, of plain talk and personal conference, but he was much more irresistible, through his kinship with academic life and his contagious charm. He asked much of young men, and the more he asked the more they gave.

Something had to be done after Drummond had departed to give utterance to the motives he had stirred, and the immediate consequence of his brief visit was a sufficient evidence of its effect. A group of undergraduates, by their own initiative and at their own expense, undertook a series of popular meetings in Boston which might carry the message of Drummond to those less fortunate than university men. They engaged a conspicuous theatre, enlisted the coöperation of the University preachers and choir, and with a surprising understanding of group psychology, instead of opening the doors to all and thereby receiving curiosity-seekers or church-goers, organized committees which distributed tickets in the workshops and commercial establishments of Boston, and thereby secured an audience completely unacademic and largely unchurched. The theatre on five successive evenings made a scene which would have touched Drummond's heart. On the stage, and framed in a Forest of Arden background, sat a chorus of more than a hundred students, with the choir of men and boys which had become distinguished for its excellence at the University Chapel; while other students ushered in a motley company of workers and wanderers. Printed lists of familiar hymns were distributed and the choir and chorus led the singing. Each member of the Staff of University Preachers took his turn in leading the worship and in addressing the assembly, and on each evening the theatre was filled with two thousand or more uneducated and diversified, but reverent and responsive, listeners. It was, of course, not a thoroughgoing or adequate invasion of the great city; the busy life of college students could not detach itself altogether from its own work; but it was at least a significant gesture of communal responsibility, as though these young men had taken to heart the outward-looking and healthy-minded words which Drummond had more than once recalled to them, 'For their sakes I sanctify myself.' Drummond's biographer has graciously reproduced a letter in which I reported 'the substantial good which has remained of your week among us here. Movements of the deepest interest have sprung from the impulse you gave, and I date from the beginning of last year a larger sense of religious responsibility.'

Such, at one point among many, was the effect created by Drummond's hasty journeys among the American universities. It was as though a comet had flashed upon the view and had left a trail of light as it sank below the horizon. It must have been with something of this effect that Drummond's Teacher journeyed through the villages of Galilee, teaching from the hillside or the boat, playing with

Present-Day Saints

the children, interpreting the lessons of the sheep and the leaven, and speaking great words of such consolation and reassurance that those who heard them said to one another, 'Did not our hearts burn within us while he talked with us by the way?' If a saint must be a stern, grim, and ascetic figure, with a visible halo and a dehumanized manner of life, then Henry Drummond cannot be counted among the beatified; but if there is room among the 'holy' for joy in life, for courage in adventure, for delight in God, and for the beauty of holiness, then this gallant, gracious, guileless gentleman, whom his companions called a Prince, should be long remembered among the saints of the modern world.

These Services will be held on Dec. 11, 18, 25, and Jan. 8 and 15.
The Preachers to the University are

Rev. E. E. Hale, D.D.
Rev. Phillips Brooks, D.D.
Rev. Alexander McKenzie, D.D.
Rev. Francis G. Peabody, D.D.
Rev. George A. Gordon.

ADMIT THE BEARER
TO THE
RELIGIOUS SERVICES AT GLOBE THEATR

SUNDAY EVENING, DEC. 18, 1887.

MEETINGS CONDUCTED BY THE STUDENTS OF HARVARD COLLEGE, ADDRESSED BY THE PREACHERS TO THE UNIVERSITY. MUSIC BY THE COLLEGE CHOIR AND A CHORUS OF STUDENTS.

Doors open at 7 o'clock. Services begin at 7.30 o'clock. *See other $*

CHAPTER XI

CARL HILTY

THE third personality which has illustrated to me the range and diversity of academic intimacies was as remote in circumstances and vocation from Armstrong and Drummond as they were from each other. The first was an American, the second a Scotchman, the third a Swiss. The first was a soldier turned teacher; the second a man of leisure turned preacher; the third a jurist turned mystic. Nothing could be more surprising than Armstrong's genius for educational reform, unless it were Drummond's abrupt conversion to missionary work, or a professor of jurisprudence becoming a spiritual seer.

It was in the year 1891, when I was in Germany on sabbatical leave, that I happened to have my attention called to a little volume just published, with the alluring title, 'Happiness.' It contained essays on such inviting themes as 'The Art of Work,' 'Good Habits,' 'How to fight Life's Battles,' 'The Art of having Time.' The collection had already been very widely welcomed by German readers. Its circulation had reached sixty thousand copies, and translations were announced into French, Dutch, Danish, Hungarian, and other languages. The essays proved, on a hasty reading, to exhibit a blend-

ing of worldly wisdom and meditative mysticism, as
of a man of wide experience but of sustained faith,
with a sanity which could see life as it is and a
serenity which could see it steadily and whole.
Quite to my surprise, I learned that what seemed
the reflections of a recluse were in fact the by-
products of a man concerned with large affairs, a
professor of international law, and a member of
the Swiss Legislature.

The impression made by this striking fusion of
learning and charm, of common sense and vision,
was so great that I entered into correspondence
with the author, and soon made a pilgrimage to
Berne, where I was received with a gracious, not
to say courtly, hospitality. I found a tall, erect, and
soldierly figure, with no trace of a scholar's habits
or of academic reserve, and giving the impression
of a retired officer rather than of a mystic or idealist.
Hilty had, in fact, in the course of the military service
prescribed for all Swiss citizens, risen to the rank
of colonel, and had sat as chief justice in the military
court. His lodging, on the other hand, was extremely
modest, and his way of life, as a widower with one
devoted daughter, was obviously Spartan. He was
a total abstainer, both from alcohol and from tobacco,
and this had set him quite apart from convivial
colleagues and clubs. It was a singular union of
refinement and simplicity, of manifestly ascetic
tastes and not less manifest dignity and authority.

Yours very truly
C. Hilty

Carl Hilty

He entered cordially into my plan of translating into English the little book I had just read, and I proceeded at once with what proved to be by no means an easy task. Hilty's literary style is idiomatic and epigrammatic, and not infrequently, it would seem, unstudied and hasty; and it was a comfort to read, years later, that he had been doubtful whether it would bear translation, and especially discouraged the attempt to translate it into French. It was necessary to prefix to my translation an apologetic paragraph, acknowledging much shifting of phrase and rupture of sentences; and expressing the hope that these liberties and omissions did not obscure the insight, sagacity, humor, and devoutness of which the book was evidence.[1] The publishers had more confidence than I in the reception probable for so didactic a volume; apparently realizing that many persons like to read about happiness, even if they do not intend to take the road that leads to it. Nearly twenty thousand copies were sold by them within a few years; but their anticipations slackened as mine were encouraged, and they allowed the book to go out of print in 1916, concluding, apparently, that the public had been supplied with as much happiness as the traffic would bear.

[1] *Happiness: Essays on the Meaning of Life.* The Macmillan Company, 1903. A Second Series: *The Steps of Life: Further Essays on Happiness*, was translated by Melvin Brandow, Macmillan, 1907.

Present-Day Saints

Much more profound, however, than the impression made on me by this collection of essays was that of spiritual distinction in the man himself. My pilgrimage to Berne was rewarded by a long interview in Professor Hilty's home, and a still longer walk with him through the beautiful suburbs of the city; and finally in a considerable correspondence. I had never before found myself in the presence of so complex a personality — a man of the world who was at the same time a contemplative mystic; an experienced publicist who maintained an unperturbed pietism; an erudite scholar whose talk testified to an inner life of tranquil faith. Sagacity and humor, gravity and vivacity succeeded each other in his conversation as sunlight breaks through drifting clouds. He told of his long and intimate association with the Temperance Movement in Switzerland, known as the 'Blue Cross'; he discoursed of personal religion as distinguished from institutional conformity; and it was difficult to believe that with another companion he might have been discussing constitutional law or Swiss legislation

To live for twenty years in the environment of national politics and academic administration, lecturing on the principles of government, sitting in the National Legislature, editing a journal of Swiss jurisprudence, and at the same time to maintain the habit of grave reflection and lofty idealism;

Carl Hilty

to be thus at once a publicist and a recluse — all this seemed to set Professor Hilty quite by himself among the public men of his generation. His contributions to learning had given him an assured place among European scholars; but seen at close range they proved to be only the professional occupations of a 'spiritually minded man of the world.' The onerous obligations of a legislator, editor, and professor had not blinded his spiritual vision. The wisdom which he applied to affairs of government was what the Christian apostle described as the 'wisdom from above.' It was a dramatic and refining experience to venture into the presence of a learned professor and find him a serene and gracious saint.

CARL HILTY was born in 1833 at Werdenberg, a village in the Swiss Canton of St. Gallen.[1] He was the son of a much respected physician and of a gifted mother whose family had long lived in Chur. The schools of the Canton were severely administered, with hours of instruction from seven in the

[1] Hilty's career is described with the fervor of an ardent disciple by H. Auer, *Carl Hilty, Blätter zur Geschichte Seines Lebens ur* : *Wirkens*, 1910, and with more academic restraint by Professor W. Burkhardt, Hilty's successor as editor of the *Polit. Jahrbuch der Schweiz. Eidgenossenschaft*, Bd. XXIV. 1910, s. 405 ff. The same issue contains a bibliography of Hilty's writings (pp. 415 ff.), and, by a touching coincidence, Hilty's last essay, published posthumously, and applying the principle of Kant's essay on Peace (*Zur ewigen Friede*, 1795) to the new conditions of the world, under the title *Pax Perpetua*.

morning to noon and from one to seven in the evening, and home studies from which, as Hilty later recalled, he was seldom free before midnight. Reading one day the aphorism of Richard Rothe, 'He is a happy man who when he lies down at night rejoices at the thought of rising the next morning,' Hilty annotated the passage with the pathetic reminiscence: 'By this test the pupils in the schools of Chur were seldom happy.' In 1851, when eighteen years of age, with a disciplined mind but an undeveloped body, Hilty migrated to the universities of Germany as a student of jurisprudence, first at Göttingen, and later at Heidelberg under von Mohl, receiving his doctorate there in April, 1854, with a dissertation on the principles of criminal law. Armed with this testimony to his scholarship, he proceeded, first to London, and then to Paris, learning the languages and delighting in the opportunities for research in the libraries and archives. Returning to Chur in 1855, he lived for eighteen years the inconspicuous but contented life of a practicing attorney in his native Canton, winning the confidence of his community and finding time for discursive reading.

His visit to England had kindled an interest in Carlyle and Tennyson, and his classical studies had led him to intimacy with the teachings of Marcus Aurelius and of Epictetus, by both of whom his later thought was profoundly affected. It was, in

Carl Hilty

short, a period of slow ripening in power, under favoring conditions of modest usefulness and with leisure for thoughtful meditation. 'If I had to choose,' he later said, 'I should wish my life to begin again as before.' In 1857, he was happily married to the daughter of a German professor of jurisprudence; of whom, after her death, twenty years later, he wrote: 'If there be a future life, I could wish to meet no one with such unmeasured joy as the wife I have had here. She was a part of my innermost and best life, which since her departure has never been complete.'

This tranquil and provincial life was in 1873 brought to an abrupt conclusion. Hilty had used some leisure hours in writing a pamphlet on 'Theorists and Idealists of Democracy' (1868), which had attracted the attention of the political leaders of Switzerland, and led to his appointment as professor of jurisprudence at the University of Berne. From this point Hilty's career became one of conspicuous service and abundant literary productiveness, until, after thirty-five years of academic life, he became known as the Nestor of the University. In 1875 he published his 'Ideas and Ideals of Swiss Politics'; in the same year his lectures on the 'Political Character of the Swiss Federation'; and in 1878 his 'Public Lectures on the Principles of Switzerland,' all designed to reënforce the movement toward democracy. In 1879 appeared his protest against capital punishment, 'On the Proposed Restoration of the Death Penalty.' In 1889 he became deeply concerned with the problem of international peace, and published in rapid succession his 'Swiss Neutrality'; and 'Eternal Peace,' revised and reissued under the title 'Pax Perpetua,' in 1909. More notable and laborious was his prolonged service as editor for twenty-three years, from 1886 until his death in 1909, of the 'Year Book of Swiss Politics,' a voluminous publication of from six hundred to seven hundred pages annually, containing elaborate studies of legislative, social, and literary events, with contemporary documents and notices of citizens of importance who had died during each year. The greater part of this material was written by Hilty himself, and the work remains a monument of industry and information.

Such, in brief outline, is an indication of the scope of Hilty's academic and political career. He was twice Rector of the university, in 1880 and 1890; he was a delegate to the World Court at The Hague; he was given a doctor's degree at the three hundredth anniversary of the University of Geneva. It was an arduous term of statesmanship and authorship, which would seem to make a sufficient record of a public-spirited and productive life.

This official and editorial service does not, however, represent the permanent influence exercised on his countrymen and the world by this remarkable

man. His political writings and his participation
in parliamentary debates had in some degree revealed
a deeper faith which cared more for the inner character of a country than for its external security.
By degrees, this desire to explore and strengthen
the spiritual sources of national welfare took firmer
hold of his mind, and in 1891 he began the series of
short studies of life and duty which make his permanent gift to posterity. The first collection,
'Happiness' (1891), was, as has been already said,
at once recognized as striking, with a light touch, a
new note of teaching; and was reviewed with enthusiasm by critics as far removed from each other, and
from the author, as St. Petersburg and St. Louis.
The same popular welcome greeted a second series
of similar papers (1895), of which forty-five thousand
copies were promptly sold; and a third volume
(1899), with a sale of thirty thousand copies. Close
upon this series of sane counsels, followed in quick
succession treatises on 'Reading and Speaking' (1895);
'Good Manners' (1898), and two studies concerned
with the nervous disorders which were beginning to
afflict modern life, 'Neurasthenia' (1897), and 'Sick
Souls' (1907). There should be noticed also a comforting collection of aphorisms for invalids, entitled
'For Sleepless Nights' (1891), of which Hilty's
biographer reports the sale of thirty thousand
copies. To this diversified list were later added,
besides many other brief discourses, two volumes of

Present=Day Saints

'Letters' (1903), (1906), addressed to anonymous correspondents; and in Hilty's last year a striking commentary on the problems of life and death under the title 'Eternal Life' (1908). The circulation of these brief and often hastily written meditations and counsels is estimated by Hilty's biographer as reaching the astonishing total of three hundred thousand copies; and this almost unprecedented popularity of so unassuming and detached an observer of life is a sufficient evidence that he had found an entrance into many minds which neither Church nor Scripture nor severely didactic literature had been able to reach.

The teachings which recur in all these treatises are singularly uniform, not to say reiterated. They are the counsels and admonitions of a man of large experience and ripened wisdom, completely devoid of literary ambition, who sets the great aims of life in true perspective over against its minor incidents, and whose touches of irony and humor induce in the reader, not protest, but smiling consent. Scholars and uninstructed minds alike see without offence their own thoughts and foibles as in a mirror, and the problems of their own experience interpreted without exaggeration or disguise. The very titles of Hilty's chapters have this note of intimacy and insight: — 'What is Culture?' 'Sin and Sorrow,' 'On the Knowledge of Men,' 'Noble Souls,' 'The Steps of Life,' 'Modern Saintliness,' 'Worship,'

Carl Hilty

'For and Against Women.' Detached paragraphs do not easily suggest the mingled playfulness and gravity which are met on every page. Each essay begins with unimportant details of conduct or thought, and slips so lightly into its spiritual lesson that one may fancy himself reading an entertaining commentary on modern society and find it, without warning, a sermon.

Thus in defining the 'Art of Work' he begins with the most elementary suggestions: 'What is the difficulty which chiefly hinders work? It is laziness. Every man is naturally lazy. It always costs one an effort to rise above one's customary condition of physical indolence. Moral laziness is, in short, our original sin. No one is naturally fond of work; there are only differences of natural and constitutional excitability. Even the most active-minded, if they yielded to their natural disposition, would amuse themselves with other things rather than with work. . . . Thus it happens that while ambitious and self-seeking people are often very diligent workers, they are seldom continuous and evenly progressive workers. They are almost always content with that which looks like work, if it produce favorable conditions for themselves, although it does nothing for their neighbors. Much of our mercantile and industrial activity — and alas! we must add, much of the work of scholars and artists — has this mark of unreality. . . .

Present-Day Saints

'There remain a few elementary rules with which one can the more easily find his way to this habit of work. And first among such rules is the knowledge how to begin. The resolution to set one's self to work and to fix one's whole mind on the matter in hand is really the hardest part of working. When one has once taken his pen or his spade in hand, and has made the first stroke, his work has already grown easier. There are people who always find something especially hard about beginning their work, and who are always so busy with preparations, behind which lurks their laziness, that they never apply themselves to their work until they are compelled; and then the intellectual and even the physical excitement roused by the sense of insufficient time in which to do one's work injures the work itself.'

From these comments on conduct Hilty soon passes to reflections on the present and the future: 'Only he who works knows what enjoyment and refreshment are. Rest which does not follow work is like eating without appetite. The best, the pleasantest, and the most rewarding — and also the cheapest — way of passing the time, is to be busy with one's work. And as matters stand in the world to-day it seems reasonable to anticipate that at the end of our century some social revolution will make those who are then at work the ruling class; just as at the beginning of the last century a social revolution gave to industrious citizens their victory over the idle nobility and the idle priests. Wherever any social class sinks into idleness, subsisting, like those idlers of the past, on incomes created by the work of others, there such nonproductive citizens again must yield. The ruling class of the future must be the working class.'

Again, in writing on the 'Art of Having Time,' he deals, first, with the waste of time: 'In this enumeration of the things which waste one's time, I may add that one must not permit himself to be over-burdened with superfluous tasks. There are in our day an infinite number of these — correspondence, committees, reports, and, not the least, lectures. All of them take time, and it is extremely probable that nothing will come of them. When the Apostle Paul was addressing the Athenians, he remarked that they did nothing else than to hear some new thing. It was not the serious part of his address, or its spiritual quickening, to which they gave their attention, it was its novelty; and the outcome of his sermon was simply that some mocked, and the most friendly said with patronizing kindness, "We will hear thee again of this matter." Indeed, the reporter of the incident finds it necessary to mention expressly that one member of the Athenian City Council and one woman in the audience received some lasting good from the Apostle's address. How is it, let me ask you, with yourselves? Have the lectures which you have heard been to you

in any way positive contributions to your insight
and decision, or have they been merely the evidence
of the speaker's erudition?' and he concludes: 'The
true spirit of work, which has not time for super-
fluities, but time enough for what is right and true,
grows best in the soil of that philosophy which sees
one's work extending into the infinite world, and
one's life on earth as but one part of life itself. Then
one gets strength to do his highest tasks, and patience
among the grave difficulties and hindrances which
confront him, both within himself and in the times
in which he lives. One is calmly indifferent to much
which in the sight of this world alone may seem
important, but which, seen in the light of eternity,
loses significance. This is the meaning of that
beautiful saying of the philosopher of Görlitz [Jacob
Böhme], which brings to our troubled time its
message of comfort:

> '"He who, while here, lives the eternal life
> Is through eternity set free from strife."'

Or, once more, in 'The Steps of Life,' he begins:
'Every life has steps; and no life runs from beginning
to end in unchanging uniformity, like a clear, mur-
muring meadow-brook, or in a straight direction,
like an artificially contrived canal.' He then passes
from one phase of experience to another with their
successive problems, until at last he reaches their
religious significance: 'The special task of the final

step of life is to live, in all sincerity, in nearness to God — something that it is much easier to think of than to describe. . . . To begin with, there will usually come a great and final trial; for all men in whom God takes a real interest (if we may so speak) must again and again, in the different periods of their life, pass anew into a kind of smelting fire, whose glow, as Dante says, alone brings the spirit to its maturity, and separates it from the inferior elements of its nature. . . . If he pass through this without ever losing his trust in God, then he has approached nearer to the divine than could happen in any other way; and if there is such a thing as a life of blessed spirits after the fashion of our present feelings and conceptions, then he will be brought so near to this by acquiring such a temperament that a transition to that life will now appear conceivable and possible.'

It was inevitable that a writer so serenely self-confident and so indifferent to scholastic methods — and especially, as in Hilty's case, one who became so extraordinarily popular — should encounter drastic criticism; and these depreciations of his teaching were soon forcibly expressed from two points of view. On the one hand, the theologians observed the lack both of positive dogma and of concern for institutional religion; and one German professor went so far as to describe Hilty's writings under the title, 'The Fear of Thinking' ('Schlatter, *Die Furcht*

vor dem Denken,' 1900). 'The world,' Hilty had
said, 'is satiated with theological dogmas, and hun-
gers and thirsts, not for new systems or philosophies,
but for realities which have happened or are happen-
ing. The modern man cares little for the theological
questions which have preoccupied subtle minds ever
since the time of Christ, and have even been the
cause of bloody wars. He is not concerned about
the mysteries of Christ's preëxistence and double
nature, or the effect of his sacrificial death on the
redemption of the world.' Such announcements
appeared to the defender of orthodox ·theology a
sheer abnegation of the reasoning faculty, a 'fear
of thinking,' and at considerable length he pressed
the claims of doctrinal foundations for faith. It
was a renewal of the perennial controversy between
the logicians and the mystics, a protest against con-
trasting theology with life, or subordinating historical
proofs to personal experience.

Hilty, in short, must be given his place in the long
and beautiful tradition of Christian mysticism. His
view of the supernatural and the miraculous, and his
principles of exegesis, are almost childlike in their
simplicity. What concerns him is the life of God in
the soul of man, the practice of the presence of God.
When he reports the personalities and prophets who
have meant most to him he names the Apostle
John, Dante, Thomas à Kempis, Tauler, Cromwell;
and of modern characters, Carlyle, Blumhardt,

Carl Hilty

Mrs. Booth, and Tolstoi — the last 'with points of strong dissent!' Not one of these was a theologian or an institutionalist. All represent the religion of experience, the direct communion of the soul with the Eternal.

Most intimate and continuous in his devotion to Dante, whom he repeatedly cites; and of whom, in one of his letters he says: 'Dante has been to many, and, in a time like ours, when others can find no way out of the Wild Wood of care and doubt, is a guide to nobler living. . . . His readers may be at first overmastered by the positive beauty of the verse, but will come at last to see that the consciousness of God is the only solution of the problem of life.'

Hilty, then, with the whole gracious company of the mystics, must accept the disapproval of the traditionalist and ecclesiastic, and be contented with the loyalty of those who have some glimpse of the vision which is so plain to him. 'The difference,' he says, 'between ordinary piety and mysticism is that the first looks to religion to make life happier, and the second finds happiness in religion itself. The first want as much of God as is necessary, the second as much as is possible.' 'The inner life of man,' he says again, 'always has in it this element of mysticism. It cannot be interpreted by biology or psychology, but reveals itself only to experience. When a witness before a judge begins to tell of his opinions, the judge interrupts him and says, "We

want to know what you have seen or heard." What
the world now wants is not dogmas, but witnesses.' [1]

On the other hand, Hilty's teaching was not less
vigorously criticized from another point of view by
Friedrich Naumann, while that eloquent orator was
still a pastor, and had not felt himself forced out of
the Christian ministry into what appeared to him
the more urgent ministry of parliamentary life.[2]
Hilty, according to Naumann, approaches the
position of the Christian socialist in his teachings of
ethical and spiritual Christianity, but remains
essentially an individualist, concerned with personal
experience alone, and with no consciousness of the
new world of social agitation and reconstruction.
'Our scheme of social revolution seems to him
Utopian; he does not realize that lives must be
saved, not separately, but together; that the need
of the time is not a new dogma or a new ethics, but
a recognition of the fact that God has set us together,
and that in our own religious life we must have our
eyes open to the need of our brother. They have
the same right of thought and action as we, and we

---

[1] It has been of peculiar interest to discover that the copy of
Hilty's third series on *Happiness* in the Harvard Library, from which
these citations are made, was the property of William James, and
is freely marked in pencil by him. Citations from it appear at many
points of his own analysis of mysticism. (*Varieties of Religious
Experience*, pp. 70, 275, 472.)

[2] F. Naumann, *Einige Gedanken über die Gründung christlich-
socialer Vereine. Entgegnung auf Prof. Dr. Hilty's gleichnamigen
Vortrag*, 1896.

are to give it to them. When we better understand
the person of Jesus Christ we shall find in him the
tenderest feeling for the lives about him. The kingdom of God is revealed to babes. The joy of Jesus
is in the spiritual recognition of those who have
never before been called up higher. . . . Professor
Hilty says that we need a kind of Puritan Christianity; Professor Harnack has said that we are already
experiencing a revival of Franciscan Christianity;
to my mind these hopes are not to be contrasted,
but made one.'

Here again it must be admitted that Hilty's
message is open to criticism. If, on the one hand,
the mystic is indifferent to doctrinal theology, it is
not less true, on the other hand, that he is primarily
concerned with meditation rather than with beneficence. Hilty thus stands at the end of an era
rather than at the beginning of a new movement,
and touches but slightly the note of a socialized
Christianity. His teaching is a recall from the
elaborate systems which have obscured the 'facts'
of religion, and revives the simplicity which is in
Christ; but there is little in it which goes beyond
self-discipline and self-realization. The very word
'Happiness,' which is so conspicuous in Hilty's
teaching, has in it something which fails to satisfy
the new spirit of social service and sacrifice. Hilty
thus meets in an extraordinary degree the needs of
the discouraged, the timid, and the self-distrustful,

as though the word of the Hebrew prophet were
spoken again: 'He giveth power to the faint; and
to them that have no might he increaseth strength';
but he does not speak to those who find in happiness
an inadequate, not to say an unworthy, ideal, and
who have heard the greater message of self-forgetful
love, 'For their sakes I sanctify myself.'

Such seem to be the most important contributions, and the most obvious limitations, of this
serene and gracious master. To many readers his
calm reflections may appear lacking in aggressive
and organized initiative. Such minds are more
inclined to look out than to look in. Their religion
is one that lends a hand. Happiness is to them less
admirable than efficiency. There are, however,
many minds — and perhaps it is true of all thoughtful people in some of their deeper experiences
of sorrow or doubt — that find in the literature
of Christian mysticism a singular support and restraint. There is a timeless virtue in Thomas à
Kempis and Fénelon, in the sermons of Tauler and
the 'Theologia Germanica.' 'The consciousness,'
as William James has said, 'that the conscious
present is continuous with a wider self through
which saving experience comes'; the discovery, as
Rufus Jones has taught, that 'we cannot live a
moment without being more than ourselves; . . .
we make all advances by trusting the soul's invisible
surmise; . . . we keep seeking God because we are

I shall be very happy to see
you again once more in this life.
        Believe me always yours
                very sincerely & truly

27 may. 78   C. Hilty

Carl Hilty

all the time finding Him' — all these profound experiences of self-discovery and self-surrender make their appeal, perhaps more than ever, to the busy life of the modern world. 'It is a blessed thing,' Phillips Brooks, with generous sympathy, testified, 'that in all times there have always been men to whom religion has not presented itself as a system of doctrine, but as an elemental life, in which the soul of man came into very direct and close communion with the soul of God. It is the mystics of every age who have done most to blend the love of truth and the love of man within the love of God. . . . The mystic spirit has been like a deep and quiet pool in which tolerance, when it has been growing old and weak, has been again and again sent back to bathe itself and to renew its youth and vigor.'

In commenting on the character of Cardinal Mercier, the Anglo-Catholic mystic, Evelyn Underhill, has lately said: [1] 'In Cardinal Mercier a solid intellectualism was closely allied to a lofty spirituality. He possessed the really scientific temper, with its love of the concrete, its distrust of abstractions, its docility to facts. . . . This, however, is but one aspect of a nature which combined in a remarkable degree the qualities of a contemplative philosopher and a man of action, and whose arduous intellectual and administrative work was simply the outward expression of a life lived in the presence of eternity.'

[1] *London Spectator*, December 4, 1926.

Something of this might be said of Hilty. He was a man of action who lived in the presence of eternity. Discerning and sagacious as are his comments on the habits and follies of modern life, his permanent place is among the interpreters of spiritual experience. The legislation of Switzerland owes much to his academic service; but great numbers of lives, both in his own and in other countries, ensnared in doubts and fears, in self-distrust or self-conceit, owe much more to the sanity of his counsels and the simplicity of his faith.

I have already indicated the singular blending of gracious refinement and missionary ardor which impressed one in the personality of Henry Drummond. Something of the same sense of contrasted qualities and resulting symmetry was the effect of acquaintance with Hilty. The academic teacher was at the same time a spiritual seer. The man of the world was at heart a mystic. The two portraits of Hilty which I have been tempted to insert represent these two aspects of his character. In the one he is the gallant and brilliant gentleman; in the other he has become, in later life, the grave, white-bearded recluse; but in both there is the same look of spiritual nobility, the same commanding personality, the same searching gaze. His bearing and manner were those of a modern publicist; his conversation and counsels were those of a present-day saint.

CHAPTER XII

LOUISA AND GEORGINA SCHUYLER

THERE remains to be added to these reminiscences of academic life, and of association with counsellors and guides in the larger world, a brief record of intimacies identified with the last period of a long life, when the pressure of routine was relaxed and more time could be rescued from absorbing, and often unprofitable, occupations.

My dear friend and neighbor William James warmly advised withdrawal from service of the University while one retained his faculties and his disposition to work; and, concurring in this judgment, I presented my resignation on my sixty-fifth birthday, with the consoling consciousness that at least it was offered before it was demanded. The title of 'Emeritus Professor' had always suggested to my mind a honorific appointment, which carried a gesture of academic appreciation; but I was rash enough to consult a Latin dictionary on the subject, and was chastened to learn that the word was defined in less flattering terms. 'Emeritus,' it appeared, signified, at its best, 'a soldier who has served out his time,' 'an exempt'; and in its secondary sense, in even less flattering language, 'unfit for service,' 'worn out,' *e.g.*, '*apes fessæ et jam emeritæ*' (Pliny); '*aratrum*' (Ovid); '*acus*' (Iuvenal).

Present-Day Saints

Neither a tired bee nor a worn-out plough nor a blunt needle, seemed to indicate a congratulatory appellation; and satisfaction had to be found in 'exemption from service,' mitigated by the timely beneficence of Mr. Carnegie.

The blessed freedom thus attained from the bondage of term-time and classroom permitted a longer residence in the seclusion of a summer home; and it happened that, by singular good fortune, that home had been established among the richest resources both of nature and of companionship. The island of Mt. Desert, on the coast of Maine, was for many years so difficult of access that it remained a resort of few visitors except nature-lovers and artists. By degrees the tide of fashion and luxury swept over its Eastern shore, but for a time left unsubmerged the more rugged coast to the Westward, where plainer ways of living attracted impecunious ministers and 'emeriti' professors to colonization. A remarkable group was soon gathered in and about Northeast Harbor. President Eliot had settled on one headland and Bishop Doane on the opposite shore, and there soon arrived some of the wisest of college presidents, the most beloved of clergymen, and the most congenial of friends. It was jestingly said in those days that at Bar Harbor one was asked how much he owned, and at Northeast Harbor how much he knew; and the simplicity of President Eliot's habit of life on one side of the harbor, together

Louisa Lee Schuyler.

with the pastoral affection of Bishop Doane on the other, established a tradition of refinement and restraint which even under later conditions of luxurious living is still perceptible and commanding. Many a casual tourist is surprised to find one summer resort left where everybody goes to church in the morning, where the young people gather from the hills and the sea for a 'Sunset Service,' and where both summer visitors and village folk crowd the little theatre in the evening for their 'Sunday Evening Club.'

It would be pleasant to write of many 'saints,' both men and women, for whom the beauty of nature has been a fit environment for beautiful lives. Pastors and teachers, authors and publicists, gracious and brilliant women, kindly hosts and distinguished guests, throng in one's memory, and might have been met at any turn of the trails or on any headland on the bay. It is sufficient, however, to recall two homes among my neighbors, one of summer residents and one of a plain villager, which may illustrate, both by their diversity and their spiritual likeness, the character of this community, and may incline a visitor to say with the Apostle Paul, 'We are no more strangers and foreigners, but fellow-citizens with the saints.'

By a singular coincidence, these two homes, thus associated with recent years, revive also the memory of intimacies begun more than a half-century ago,

255

and have provided, not only cheering companionship in age, but a happy reminiscence of youth. No early acquaintance beyond my family circle is more vivid in memory than that with Louisa and Georgina Schuyler; no incident is more definitely the starting-point of my professional life than my first meeting with Frederic Phillips. To find these friends of many years ago among my nearest neighbors, on the shore of what a poet has called 'The harbor of dreams' was to recall my own early dreams opening out into broader experiences as the narrow harbor opened out into the sea.

My first acquaintance with Louisa and Georgina Schuyler was of the most casual character, but soon led to a friendship, interrupted by intervals of separation and silence, but always renewed with a sense of mutual understanding and intimacy. It happened that friends of my parents, whom I was taught to call, after the New England fashion, Uncle and Aunt, lived at Irvington-on-the-Hudson, and as a little boy I was permitted to visit them in their lovely home. Indeed, I was less than ten years old when first received by these pseudonymous relations; for I find among my archives the autograph of their neighbor, Washington Irving, dated 'Sunnyside, June 10, 1857, written for Master F. G. Peabody.' These friends of my family had found no congenial place of worship in their neighborhood, and had therefore been led to establish, for their children and

Louisa and Georgina Schuyler

for any neighbors who sympathized with their Unitarian tradition, an informal meeting for family worship. The guests sat in a circle in the large living-room, each reading a verse of scripture, and all led in prayer by the master of the house. To this little gathering the sisters known as 'the Schuyler girls' made it their practice to come with their mother, and I was soon permitted to visit them repeatedly in their picturesque home a few miles down the river. Later, by a happy accident, on our wedding journey, my wife and I fell in with these sisters and their delightful father at a hotel in Pisa, and the sense of intimacy was revived as we surveyed together the most beautiful single group of architectural monuments in the world. A little later the sisters surprised us by proposing that we should join them in establishing a summer colony near Newport; and a few years later — this plan having failed — they settled themselves directly across the inlet of Northeast Harbor, and became to the end of their lives among the nearest and dearest of my neighbors.

A further evidence of affection reached me when the two sisters died, — a bequest, mutually made and identical in form, of the books and pictures gathered in their summer home. I had always imagined that the relation between us was one of admiring devotion on my part and of kindly acceptance of it on theirs; but to receive after their death

257

these well-worn volumes, chiefly of verse, and finally to be summoned to New York to assist in conducting the funerals, first of the younger, and three years later, of the elder, made a touching assurance of reciprocal attachment, which had continued for nearly seventy years.

The end of these lives must be described as nothing less than the end of an era. No Americans, so far as I know, are left who represent so completely, both by inheritance and by character, the finest traits of the Victorian age. There was in both a singular charm and nobility of nature which made them the centre of attraction for a large circle of devoted friends, both old and young. Their modest cottage at Northeast Harbor had about it an atmosphere of quiet dignity, and their hospitality a kind of gentle courtliness, which gave to many a guest the sense of entering what had seemed a departed world of serenity and restraint. Yet these Victorian ladies were by no means mere survivals of a vanishing type; but, on the contrary, very modern in their sympathies and hopes, enlisted in all the good works of their time, eager for the last news of public events, and by no means above enjoying kindly gossip. No two women were more dissimilar in inclination and taste, yet none were ever more dependent on each other, or essential for each other's happiness. Louisa was a dynamo of administrative force; Georgina was a poetic and tranquil soul. Louisa became

Louisa and Georgina Schuyler

recognized as a daring pioneer in social service; Georgina, on the other hand, was the devoted caretaker and serene companion, who lightened the burden of official duties and tranquillized the unremitting activity of her sister's career. No one who had the privilege of intimacy can think of the two sisters apart. Georgina's quietude of mind was an essential factor in Louisa's untiring energy. The wide recognition of Louisa's distinction has hid from public observation the sister's solicitude and sagacity; but those who loved them recall, in the very diversity of their characters, a perfect unity of mutually sustaining wills.

Louisa Lee Schuyler was born in 1837, and her sister Georgina four years later. They were the direct descendants of General Philip Schuyler and of Alexander Hamilton, and grew up among the traditions of this distinguished lineage. Their childhood was spent on the spacious estate of their grandfather, James Hamilton, with its great house 'Nevis,' overlooking the Hudson River and its smaller 'Cottage,' built by their father, George Lee Schuyler, in 1840, on the bank of the river, and the home of his family for forty years. James Hamilton, the grandfather, was much concerned with public affairs, and defended the career of his father, Alexander, with unqualified veneration. Although of the moderate party in the issue between the States, he had given shelter to a fugitive slave and had permitted his escape to Canada. His wife was a skilled musician; had spoken Italian from childhood; had heard Grisi in her prime, and inherited the charm of a French grandmother. George Schuyler's wife, Eliza Hamilton, died in 1863, and her daughter Georgina, the poet of the family, wrote of her:

> 'You of the noble forehead,
> You of the deep-set eyes,
> With sweet voice, eager to question,
> Or low in grave replies;
> Out of your life eternal,
> Full and joyous and free,
> Your thoughts fly back to the Cottage
> You love and remember with me.'

In 1869 Mr. Schuyler married Mary Hamilton, the younger sister of his first wife; but she remained to the daughters their beloved Aunt Mary — a vivacious and charming woman — ' the cleverest woman I ever knew,' one critical observer pronounced her.

When the war between the States began in 1861, Louisa was twenty-four years old, and Georgina twenty. Both had been bred in the inner circle of New York society, with every temptation to lives of intellectual cultivation or of self-indulgence. Their minister in New York, Henry W. Bellows, had, however, dedicated his tremendous energy and eloquence to the work of the United States Sanitary Commission, of which he became President, and in the early days of that colossal enterprise summoned

Louisa Schuyler to his aid. The call to service revealed the girl's gifts for administration and leadership, and recalled the qualities of her ancestors. She turned from a life of leisure to one of extraordinary efficiency, which persisted not only through the war but for more than sixty years.

It is difficult to visualize the condition of national affairs which prompted this vast organization of private relief, of which the Red Cross of the present time is the lineal successor. The first contingent of Northern troops had been hurried precipitately into service, with no adequate provision for medical or sanitary care; and the mortality by disease was at first so great that competent observers predicted the loss of fifty per cent of the fighting force by the end of the first summer. The Medical Department of the United States Army at the beginning of the war consisted of a surgeon-general and twenty-six surgeons, half of whom had served for thirty years, and none of whom had served less than twenty-three years. There were no trained army nurses, no arrangements for transportation, and, worst of all, there was a tradition of conservatism at Washington which led to the distrust or rejection of aid offered by civilians.

It was the women of the North who first realized the pressing need, and among the first of their organizations was the Women's Central Relief Association of New York, of which Louisa Schuyler became a member. Soon followed, though under persistent opposition from officials, the creation of a National Commission, which forthwith made its appeal to the heart of the Nation, 'with the simple desire,' as its Secretary, Frederic Law Olmstead said, 'to secure for the men who have enlisted in this war that care which it is the duty and the law of the Nation to give them. That care is their right and, in the Government or out of it, must be given, let who will stand in the way.' Auxiliary societies to the number of 32,000 were enlisted in this expanding work, and the entire continent was roused to participation. 'History,' wrote John Stuart Mill, a far from emotional Englishman, of the achievements of the Sanitary Commission, 'has afforded no other example of so great a work of usefulness extemporized by the spontaneous self-devotion and organizing genius of a people altogether independent of the Government.'

To this gallant service Louisa Schuyler dedicated her young life; becoming chairman of the Committee on Organization, Correspondence, and Publicity, and by an untiring dissemination of letters, lectures, and reports interpreting to each community this unprecedented work. It was for her to supervise the classifying, repacking, and forwarding of thousands of boxes. 'Jams would arrive,' she wrote, 'packed with shirts, wines with underclothing, quilts with jellies.' President Lincoln, who at the outset had hesitated to commend the Sanitary Commission, was ready at last to say: 'I am not accustomed to the language of eulogy and have never studied the art of paying compliments to women; but I must say that if all that has been said by the orators and poets since the creation of the world in praise of women were applied to the women of America, it would not do them justice for their conduct during this war.'

To the administrative genius which this untrained girl of twenty-four years exhibited must be added the discovery of a gift for literary expression with which in this national emergency she found herself endowed. Her reports are not only lucid and direct but abounding in generous emotion. She seizes on the phrase used for enlistment, 'Three years or the War!' and says, in 1864, 'That old war-cry rings through our ears. Which is it? Have we enlisted for three years, or the war? The sound echoes through the mountains of East Tennessee. It penetrates to far-off Texas and sighs among the ruins of Fort Pillow. It resounds from the walls of Libby prison. We strain our ears to catch the answer. It comes, borne upon the lightest of southern breezes, — a whisper very low, very earnest, very solemn, — for the war!' And again, when the long strain was over, and her final message must be given, she writes: 'We have all tried to do our duty; but when we look back, we shall not think of how much we have done, but of how little. God has greatly blessed us in our work, — a work interwoven with prayer; and may His blessing rest upon us always.'

Such were the spirit and the executive force with which, through four tragic years, this tenderly nurtured girl gave herself to a prodigious task, sacrificing for it her health and strength as truly as any soldier in the ranks. This gallant service was, however, only the first step in Louisa Schuyler's public career. After some years of physical recuperation, she found herself recalling a casual remark made years before by the distinguished surgeon Dr. Willard Parker, as he sat after dinner in her home. 'I wish,' he had said, 'that some of you ladies would visit those hospitals when you come to town.' The sense of a Call lay in her mind until she was thirty-five years old, and she then undertook the audacious and, as it then seemed, unfeminine task of visiting and inspecting the asylums and poorhouses within her reach. In these days, when the World War has drawn young women into every form of service, and made them at home in hospitals and camps, it is not easy to realize what it meant in 1872 for a young woman of refinement to venture into the squalid conditions under which paupers and defectives, old and young, were being maintained, restrained, and even neglected or abused. Officials and politicians offered every obstacle to such a visitation. What business had this young lady of fashion to invade with her sentimental ideas the institutions of the City and State, which were not only well-directed, but very lucrative to their administrators? It was the same opposition which had been encountered by the promoters of the Sanitary Commission when they approached the authorities in Washington. Louisa Schuyler, however, was not a person to be easily thwarted in her plans, and she literally forced her way into the institutions, interviewing the inmates, investigating the kitchens and wash-rooms, and accumulating convincing evidence of maladministration and neglect. It was a case of one girl against the organized forces of the politicians; an *Athanasia contra mundum.*

It soon became evident that no individual, however daring she might be, could carry so entrenched a position, and that organization must be met by counter-organization. Louisa Schuyler, therefore, in 1872, summoned to her father's home the most trusted leaders of New York opinion, — Charles L. Brace, Charles O'Connor, William E. Dodge, Mrs. Josephine Shaw Lowell, and many others, both men and women (for Miss Schuyler never believed in segregating the work of women); and there was organized the State Charities Aid Association, of which she became the first President; remaining on its board of managers until her death, a period of fifty-four years. The title of this society pleasantly disguised its original intention. It proposed to aid in the direction of the State charities; but it was in effect an expression of distrust concerning partisan control, and was at first regarded as an intrusive critic rather than as a trusted ally. One of the most notable achievements of the Association during its long and effective service has been the overcoming of such hostility, and the acceptance of visitation by influential and unpaid observers as a contribution to Governmental efficiency.

It is not necessary to describe in detail the further adventures of this militant crusader, but some of her later achievements may be briefly enumerated. In 1874 she participated in founding the first training-school for nurses, at the Bellevue Hospital, and in 1878 the first committee for the prevention of blindness. In 1890, after years of unremitting effort, she secured a law establishing a system of State care and support, removing the insane from poor-houses, almshouses, and jails; and in 1906 the formation of the first committee in the United States for the after-care of these wards of the State. In 1907 she became a trustee of the Russell Sage Foundation. In 1915 Columbia University conferred on her the degree of LL.D., it being the first time in one hundred and sixty-one years that this honor had been given to a woman. The citation described her as 'Pioneer in the service of noble women to the State; founder of the State Charities

Louisa and Georgina Schuyler

Aid Association and of the system of visitation of State institutions by volunteer committees of citizens ; originator of the first American training-school for nurses ; initiating and successfully advocating legis-- lation for the State care of the insane ; powerfully aiding the first public movement for the prevention of blindness in little children ; worthy representative of a long line of ancestors distinguished through centuries for manifold services to city, State, and nation.' In 1923 the Roosevelt medal was awarded her, with the following eulogy : 'Miss Louisa Lee Schuyler, to whom a medal is awarded for distinguished service in the promotion of the welfare of women and children, was a pioneer in advocating and establishing reforms in the public care of the poor, the sick, the helpless, and the insane, and the principles which she promulgated fifty years ago have become the commonplaces of modern philanthropy. She laid the foundation of modern American social service, and as founder and leader of the New York State Charities Aid Association has been the guiding force behind the extraordinary achievements of its fifty years of existence.'

These evidences of appreciation make it not extravagant to describe Louisa Schuyler as the most distinguished woman of her generation in the United States, and justify a fellow-worker in saying of her : 'She knew neither hesitation, fatigue, nor discouragement . . . it was a virile philosophy, a call to action which the bravest and the best need not hesitate to respond to, and she enlisted them all under her banner.' The indomitable energy and self-control thus commemorated are sufficiently indicated by her extraordinary habit of working at night, often until five o'clock in the morning, and then turning from this concentrated activity to eight hours of refreshing sleep. In 1921 she was stricken with paralysis, and for the greater part of five years was physically disabled. Her mind and will, however, were as tireless and determined as ever, and she devised and dictated from her bed many plans of social and political reform — even so remote a cause as the change of date in convening Congress, to abbreviate the interval between election and legislation. She died in October, 1926; and it was not unfitting that at the close of the funeral the congregation sang the Battle Hymn of the Republic. She was a true soldier, in the long war against poverty, blindness, and disease; a militant general marshalling the forces of beneficence.

Meantime, her sister, gentle in voice and demeanor, unassuming but wise, shy but unafraid, gave her life and love to smooth the path of Louisa's triumphal march, and reënforced her intrepid courage with watchful solicitude. Georgina's temperamental and cultivated tastes led her into quite another world than that of administration or reform. She was widely read in literature; at home with the best of poetry, and herself a writer of verse and a composer of songs. In 1875 she published 'for private circulation' two musical compositions — one using the words of Emerson:

> 'Think me not unkind or rude
> That I walk alone in grove and glade.'

The other the lines of Byron:

> 'When we two parted
> In silence and tears.'

Both of these compositions were sentimental rather than convincing, and expressed the romanticism of a mid-Victorian writer rather than the vigor or passion of a later generation; but both were genuine in feeling, and revealed a cultivated artist and a meditative mind. Somewhat later she applied an intimate knowledge of her ancestry to the writing of a 'History of the Schuyler Mansion at Albany'; and, finally, she left a series of unpublished chapters, describing her early home at 'Nevis' and the group of notable friends which gathered there.

These fragmentary studies are more like reflective essays than historical records. It was the color of events rather than their form which interested her; the scenery of nature and life rather than things said or teachings recalled. Thus she begins one chapter: 'It is the summer of 1856. It is June. The locust trees are in blossom. The clover is ripe. The grasses are tall and feathery, and soon the sharpen-

ing of scythes will be heard. Under the poplar trees
the bobolinks are flitting from limb to limb, and in
the full noontime the quails are calling.' Throughout
Georgina's life, both in conversation and in reading,
this lyric note persisted. The books which I have inherited were almost wholly Victorian, selected by her
as essential in a summer home, and freely annotated
by her comments and criticisms. Louisa was, so far as
I know, not much of a reader; she was too busy with
administrative and epistolary cares to love or create
literature. Georgina, on the other hand, found
spiritual refreshment in returning to her books and
in reading or learning by heart her beloved poets, or
in venturing into modest versification of her own.

It has been interesting to glance through these
little volumes, now in my possession, and to observe
what passages met the approval of her sensitive mind.
Who is there left, in a world of free verse and defiant
cleverness, who sets aside, as Georgina Schuyler
did, for summer reading, Cowper, Herbert, and
Samuel Rogers as her British poets, and Bryant,
Lanier, and Poe from among Americans, not to
speak of tiny Italian editions of Dante, Petrarch,
and Alfieri? She makes marginal notes on translations from Schiller and Körner, and against the
paragraphs of Emerson's 'Representative Men,'
where he says of Shakespeare: 'The thought con-
structs the tune, so that reading for the sense will
best bring out the rhythm'; and again: 'No recipe

GEORGINA AND LOUISA LEE SCHUYLER
Northeast Harbor, Maine, 1920

can be given for the making of a Shakespeare, but the possibility of the translation of things into song is demonstrated.' One can see this gentle reader thus annotating her favorites, quite unconcerned for changes of literary fashion, and sure that the fit will survive. She endures the demands of modern New York by maintaining companionship with a culture which had become, for most of her contemporaries, either forgotten, or remembered with a condescending smile.

What a picture is thus presented of two lives, unspoiled by luxury or pride; maintaining the simplicity of genuine aristocrats; born and bred under conditions which have tempted others to distrust democracy, but remaining throughout life passionately patriotic and confidently public-spirited; the one untiringly active, the other habitually reflective; yet each reënforcing the other through the very difference of temperaments and tastes. One thinks inevitably of the Martha and Mary of the Gospels; but in this case Martha was not 'cumbered' or 'worried' about much serving, but found joy and even physical health in the great work she was doing; and Mary, though the good part she chose was to sit and listen, was always the watchful guardian of Martha among her cares.

And if, finally, it be asked what sustained these sisters, the one in her administration and the other in her meditation, and made them singularly one in heart, it must be answered that it was their complete agreement concerning the rational religion in which both alike found hope and peace. From the days when they worshipped as young girls at Irvington, in a circle which might fitly be called a 'Friends' Meeting,' to the days when their bodies, in old age, were laid at rest, there was no variation neither shadow caused by turning in the consistency and vitality of their religious faith. In one of Georgina's unpublished chapters she reports this continuous conviction, inherited by the sisters from the influence of Channing on an earlier generation, and reënforced by their mother's convictions. 'The belief in God,' Georgina writes, 'as a loving and merciful Father, for whose pity and forgiveness no atonement is necessary . . . produces a marked difference in the Unitarian attitude towards death. Death was to be met with trust and confidence. . . . The same love that attends the soul in this world will care for it in the next. . . . This was the belief of my father and mother, and into this we children were baptized.' Such was the bond which held the sisters most closely in devoted intimacy, until the same Love which had attended them in this life was trusted to care for them in the next.

Both of these sisters were, in the language of the New Testament, 'called to be saints'; but different kinds of saints are as necessary to sanctify a modern home as they were in primitive Christianity. If the older sister were to choose her patron saint, she might have turned, with her tireless beneficence, to him who wrote that faith, if it has not works, is dead. 'I will show them,' she might say with him, 'my faith by my works.' If, on the other hand, the pensive Georgina were to name her spiritual guide, she might have turned to him who wrote: 'Beloved, let us love one another: for love is of God; and every one that loveth is born of God, and knoweth God.' The fact is, however, that the followers of Saint James and those of Saint John have equal rights to be included in the Christian hierarchy; and it still remains true, as a more influential apostle than either James or John wrote, that 'the saints shall judge the world.'

CHAPTER XIII

FREDERIC ILLSLEY PHILLIPS

THE other 'Saint' whom I select from among my kindly neighbors for reminiscence was as remote in circumstances and type as would seem possible from the sheltered lives of the Schuyler sisters. While they were adorning New York society, the one administering charities and the other writing verse, he was teaching village schools in winter, and fishing in summer along the rugged coast of Maine. Yet the same happy fate which renewed an intimacy with Louisa and Georgina Schuyler at Mt. Desert led me to find there in Frederic Phillips an acquaintance of thirty years before, and revived the memory of my earliest ventures in the ministry.

It was as long ago as 1870 that, after one year of unprofitable study in the Harvard Divinity School, I was visiting friends at Bar Harbor, Maine, when the news drifted across Frenchman's Bay that the villagers at Sullivan Falls, seven miles away, would like to have worship conducted in their little red schoolhouse. With the valor of ignorance I welcomed this opportunity, and, after some negotiation with these inaccessible neighbors, who were happily unaware of my complete inexperience, considered how to reach them. There was then no steamer on the bay and no regular packet across it, and the land

274

journey round the head of tide-water was something
like thirty miles. Consultation with local skippers
led to the discovery of a fisherman who was bound
up Skillings River on Saturday, and I took passage on
his little smack ; landed on the west shore of Han-
cock Point; trudged across to the Sullivan Ferry,
and made my way on foot to the hospitable home
of the Widow Simpson, where I was lodged each
Saturday night for several weeks. The next morning
I summoned up enough courage to conduct worship
and preach for the first time. I can recall no perceptible results, except the entrance of a travelling sales-
man of patent medicine, who had hitched his horse at
the door and joined the meagre congregation. In
departing he handed me a dollar bill, remarking that
he didn't want to steal his preaching. It was the
first professional fee I ever received, though I cannot
claim that it was fairly earned.

There followed a series of Sunday meetings, of
which, so far as I know, the only memory that long
survived among the villagers was of athletic rather
than of homiletic proficiency. It was my practice to
conduct worship at Sullivan in the morning ; drive
eight miles to the town of Franklin, unlock the meeting-house, ring the bell, sing in the choir, preach
what it would be an exaggeration to call the Gospel,
drive back to Sullivan, and row seven miles across
Frenchman's Bay in a heavy boat to Bar Harbor.
A boy who would do all this for their sakes might,

it seemed to some of the villagers, be forgiven his immaturity of mind and remembered for his strength of muscle. Few of them had ever conceived of Bar Harbor as being within rowing distance.

A more vivid memory than of the preaching is that of my first voyage across the bay. The skipper turned out to be, not a sailor by profession, but a schoolmaster, of about my own age, wisely using his summer holidays in the refreshing occupation of fishing. Each morning at daybreak he would put out from Bar Harbor, and each evening clean his catch and sell it to be dried. Our talk ran naturally to my missionary intention, and he soon revealed an astonishing familiarity with the Bible, and announced himself a devoted Baptist, demonstrating to me, as was not difficult, that the only form of initiation into Christian fellowship recognized, or even imagined, by the primitive Church was by immersion. What was good enough for the first disciples, he said, and even for Jesus himself, was good enough for him. He then inquired what was to be my text, and when I told him it was the assurance given by Paul to his young friend Timothy, 'The word of God is not bound,' my companion assented warmly to this announcement of Liberal Christianity — an evidence of catholicity which seemed to me not wholly compatible with his insistence on a special and binding rite. We parted with mutual good wishes, and even his name, if I knew it, dropped altogether from my mind.

Frederic Illsley Phillips

What was my surprise, thirty years later, when the increasing luxury of Bar Harbor drove my family life to the simplicity and seclusion of Asticou, to find this pilot of my first professional excursion my nearest neighbor ; living in a modest little cottage, tending a small market garden, and supplying milk and vegetables to summer residents. I was soon to find in this secluded and unassuming man an intimate and beloved friend. He often described himself as my first parishioner ; and as we met from day to day we greeted each other with my first text as a kind of private countersign, calling out as we passed, 'The word of God is not bound !' He soon became a trustworthy ally in maintaining the little Union Church at Northeast Harbor, and for many years served on its standing committee ; not less a convinced Baptist but more a catholic-minded Christian ; and when, with another sturdy villager, Captain Manchester, he tramped up the aisle, bearing the offering of the congregation, it was a pleasant and resounding testimony of modest discipleship which many a worshipper vividly remembers. The more intimately I came to know this neighbor the more I found in him the genuine traits of the Christian character. He would stroll down to my home with the apparent purpose of selling a basket of raspberries, but, as I soon realized, with the more serious intention of a talk on the duties of man or the mystery of God. His spiritual insight had been clarified and deepened by a life close to nature and a faith nourished on the Bible; and among these reminiscences of present-day saints I must tell of this unassuming Christian, as he lived, talked, and served in a quiet corner of the great world.

FREDERIC ILLSLEY PHILLIPS was born in 1852, in Orland, Maine, of good English stock; his great-grandfather having crossed the ocean with Sir William Pepperell, and, according to family tradition, being present with that merchant, turned general, at the taking of Louisburg in 1745. His father established himself, first at Castine and later at Orland, and the boy attended the village school in the latter town and the Normal Academy in the first. Life in these settlements along the New England coast was still primitive and disciplinary. Each little village lay between the forest and the sea, and the undaunted settlers wrung a scanty livelihood from their rocky pastures, and for lucrative trade felled the timber behind them to carry to larger towns, or launched out into the deep before them for coastwise traffic or for bankfishing. Each group of homes was set at the head of tide-water, where lumber could be with least effort got to sea. When this source of business was exhausted the village life ebbed away as with the tide; and one may still trace the rotting ways which tell of the early ship-building and the neglected dams which once held the logs. Each village built its own schooners and manned them with its own boys, and when trade prospered and captains grew more daring they ventured to the West Indies or across the sea; brought back their profits and built spacious homes, which still adorn many of these old towns. Each vigorous young man felt himself called, either to the woods or to the water, and, as a rule, to both; hewing and hauling logs in winter and shipping for the South or for the Banks in summer. There were few old men who were not saluted as 'Captain,' and few young men who had not faced the gales off Cape Cod or tended their dories beyond Cape Sable.

Such was the hard school of life in which young Phillips was trained; and the little diaries kept by him as he grew up, which have been kindly put into my hands by his children, report his intermittent work at shipbuilding and his occasional cruises along the coast. Thus in 1873, at the age of twenty-one, he writes:

'*May 1.* We shall finish loading to-morrow.

'*May 2.* A nice load of sleepers, 2762.

'Got under way May 4, about six miles ENE from Duck Islands.

'*May 17.* At anchor at Provincetown. Wind NW.

'*May 18.* Got under way last night. To-day we took a squall about ten o'clock. At 9 P.M. passed Thacher's Island, Wind W.

'*May 19.* Off Seguin. Wind dying out.

'*May 20.* Abreast of Monhegan. Very light.

'*May 21.* Arriving home [Sullivan] about noon. A nice time over the falls and anchored at Franklin. Eighteen days on trip from time we left.'

The other resource, of fishing on the Banks, was not so accessible to young Phillips. It required unlimited physical strength and a passion for adventure, and he was slight of frame and more of a dreamer than a seaman. More than once he applied for a berth and was refused; and once, as he later told his children, he watched with dejection a fishing schooner sail without him, and later when she was due watched again to see her topsails above the horizon, only to learn at last that she and all her crew were lost. It was evident that a seaman's life was not his vocation. Even when he at times shipped before the mast he was indulging in reflections and meditations which were by no means maritime, and which, if they were recorded in his diary while his watch was on deck, suggest that he was rather inclined to look in than to look out. Thus on May 7, 1872, he writes:

'Out on the ocean, tossing on the restless sea; the old ocean always undulating as if some hidden monster were passing swiftly in its depths. Wind NE, fanning us gently on our course. The booms creak and strain, the vessel rolls as if restless and longing to reach its destination, and the water, as it falls in and out of the scuppers, sighs and sobs, as if it wanted to tell tales that would cause our blood to stop its course.' Soliloquies like these, as of a young

Frederic Illsley Phillips

Conrad listening to the voices of the deep, plainly indicated that the destiny of this youth must be found on the land rather than the water; and he surrendered himself finally to the modest and nomadic life of a country-school teacher.

This in its turn was no Sybaritic experience; for it involved a shifting and homeless livelihood, with short terms of employment, meagre pay, and still more inadequate provision of books and equipment. Yet this vocation left him time to think and dream, and write his diary, and even compose or copy verses of poetry. He cheerfully realized that he was not made for a sailor, and applied himself to the less exciting task of a pedagogue; beginning with high courage and hopes, but soon, as is not infrequent in sedentary occupations, tempted to despondency, introspection, and despair. Thus, in 1873, he begins his career by teaching for nine weeks on the island of Islesboro, then uninvaded by summer visitors and practically marooned in winter from the mainland. He girds himself for this enterprise as though he were going into battle, and writes in his diary, on his first day, the sanguine lines:

> 'Onward, onward, never falter
> Till the whole world shall be free,
> And let no one call God Father
> Who cannot man's brother be';

adding to this his own resolution, 'I am bound to conquer or die. What man has done man can do.'

281

Soon, however, he writes again: 'A little lonesome to-day. All things must have an end. There is a good deal of trouble in this world, and I guess I shall have my share of it.' At the end of his term he is confronted with the problem of leaving the island, and it proves to be more of a maritime adventure than a schoolmaster's farewell. On February 24 he writes: 'Got within three miles of Castine and met a lot of ice and had to come back.' On the 26th: 'In the forenoon it blew very hard; in the afternoon I tried very hard to get off, but didn't succeed. I don't know as I shall ever get off.' Finally on the 27th he makes the passage of a few miles across the arm of Penobscot Bay, and is 'very glad to get home.' 'I have my ups and downs, but enjoy as much as is possible for me in this world. Sometimes *vice versa*.'

These migrations from schoolhouse to schoolhouse made up the young man's life for nearly twenty years, and covered not less than fifty of the short terms of teaching for which village authorities were inclined to pay. It was a task which encouraged introspection and despondency, and the diary reveals days of morbid self-examination. In September, 1874, he writes: 'I spent a terrible week last week, but happily the delusion is expelled. Oh, how I wish I could live up to what I believe to be right!' Again in 1875, on successive days, he writes only single words: 'March 30. Anguish.' '31. Distress.'

Frederic Illsley Phillips

'April 1. Going under the yoke.' 'April 3. A glimmering light.' 'April 8. Peace, happiness, and hope. I have fortified myself on every hand.' And finally on June 2, 1878: 'A day long looked to. I was baptized and joined the Baptist Church. God bless it.' These alternations of spiritual depression and exaltation were at last mitigated by his marriage in 1883; but after two happy years of companionship his wife died at the birth of a child, and the husband became again an itinerant teacher. Finally, he was appointed to the school in the little hamlet of Northeast Harbor, and there, after three years of solitude, married, in 1888, the daughter of one of the most respected residents.

It was singularly fortunate that a neighborhood soon to be invaded by the luxurious habits of summer visitors had among its first settlers families of superior and self-respecting stock. Some of the Maine settlements were the refuges of castaways or drifting mariners; but along the western shore of Mt. Desert Island a remarkable group of sturdy colonists hewed out their homes from the forests, and established their families in permanent occupation. There are few communities in the United States where land has been so continuously held for four or five generations, and where the representatives of the early stock still live on their ancestral holdings. Abraham Somes built his log house at the head of the fiord now known as Somes Sound, at the point now called Somesville,

283

as early as 1762, and the family name still meets one at that pleasant village. John Manchester made his home at Northeast Harbor in 1775, and a direct descendant, bearing his name, lives there now. When, during the World War, I was permitted to preside at the hoisting of the national flag, the little boy who pulled the halyards, and whose father was the first man of the town to cross the sea as a soldier, stood on the doorstep of his great-great-grandfather's cottage, which was still occupied by the same family in direct descent.

Here it was that I found this much-wandering Ulysses, who had been my pilot thirty years before; or rather this modern 'Christian,' after his Pilgrim's Progress toward the wicket gate, where the burden 'fell from his back and was no more seen.' He had made his home, with his wife, the daughter of Captain Savage, in a small cottage hidden behind the hotel maintained by the Savage family, and which bore the name of the great Chief Asticou, whose shell heaps may still be seen near by. Here he had become a farmer in a small way, tending his crops, milking his cows, providing his neighbors with vegetables; but with time to reflect much on life, manners, and God, and with the inclination to despondency quite displaced by a happy family life, the care of devoted children, and the serenity of a genuine and controlling religious faith. So, by the happy convergence of our paths my life fell in again with that of this neighbor, generally known by the title given to most men of his age in the village as 'Captain Phillips,' though his only claim, so far as I know, to this designation was as commander and crew of his little fishing smack on Frenchman's Bay.

There is a Greek tradition reported by Cicero which tells of a visit of Pythagoras to the city of Phlius. Being asked by that Prince concerning the art to which he devoted himself, he replied that he was a philosopher. The Prince inquired wherein a philosopher differed from other men, and Pythagoras answered that human life resembled a great fair, to which some resorted to buy and sell, and others simply to look about them. 'These then are they whom I call students of wisdom, for such is meant by philosopher.' The philosopher, that is to say, is one who looks about him and sees all that is going on. I was often reminded of this definition as my neighbor Captain Phillips talked about current events. He was a philosopher, looking on at the great fair of life. His talk was, as I often thought, of just the kind that would have interested Emerson if he had fallen in with Captain Phillips at Concord, — shrewd with the sagacity of a Yankee, and serene with the composure of a Christian.

In the happy experience of a permanent home he had maintained his habit of diary-keeping; but, instead of tearing up his moods by the roots, he let them flower out in sanguine, and often playful, comments on life and duty, until the title of his last book of records read : 'Other people's thoughts and some of my own.' He sets down verses which have won his attention, like those of Maltbie Babcock :

'Why be afraid of death,
As though your life were breath?
Death but anoints the eyes
With clay — as glad surprise.

'Why should you be forlorn?
Death only husks the corn ;
Why should you fear to meet
The thresher of the wheat?'

There follow notes on the births, deaths, and genealogy of his family; poems by Will Carlton and Mary Mapes Dodge ; and finally a characteristic allusion to his birthday, occurring just after the death of his beloved and devoted wife : 'How swiftly the years go ! Seventy-three to-day. I miss Cora more and more as the days go by. To form these attachments, these intertwining affections, the gradual similarity of dissimilar tastes — and all to be disrupted. I never before realized the uncertainty of life. Perhaps life is not the word ; things temporal is a better phrase.

'"I know not where his islands lift
Their fronded palms in air ;
I only know I cannot drift
Beyond his love and care."'

Such was the self-possessed and tranquil mystic with whom I renewed a happy companionship. He

Frederic Illsley Phillips

had outgrown the feverishness of his early years, and had reached an Indian summer of spiritual tranquillity and enjoyment. In his last letter to me he wrote: 'The following lines came to me last night. I don't know whether they are mine or some one else's:

'" Unless we see His presence
In all the ways of life
We've missed and lost the meaning
Of all this endless strife."'

'From your first parishioner,
'F. I. Phillips.'

It would not be just to leave this sketch as the portrait of an idle dreamer. On the contrary, my neighbor became an active and effective member of the little community in which his last years were spent. For seventeen years he was a health-officer of the town, and a devoted adherent of the Baptist Church, and he initiated and promoted two of the most significant enterprises ever undertaken under the conditions of a summer resort in Maine. The first suggested itself to him so suddenly that it might be called an inspiration. He was sitting on my piazza on one of his friendly visitations, and, looking across the meadow to the next house, casually inquired, 'What does your next neighbor, Mr. Barnes, do for his living?' I replied that I did not know what he did for his living, but that I did know what he did with his life; and thereupon told him of the great meeting held each Sunday evening in the largest hall of Chicago, with its noble music, its famous speakers, and its prodigious popularity for many years. I told him that very few of the thousands who thronged Orchestra Hall had been in a church that day; that they were for the most part the un-churched nomads of the city — commercial travellers spending their Sundays at the neighboring hotels; young people out for a Sunday evening stroll on the boulevard ; and great numbers of persons who wanted religion but did not care for the methods and demands of the churches. Such, I told my neighbor, was the eager, responsive audience at the Sunday Evening Club. All this, I said, which made the Club one of the most remarkable religious gatherings of the world, was due to Mr. Barnes, who had devised and in-spired it.

Greatly to my surprise, Captain Phillips, instead of being overawed by the magnitude of this cosmo-politan enterprise, said, 'Why that's just what we ought to have in Northeast Harbor!' 'Why not say that to Mr. Barnes?' I suggested. 'Why not see him about it now?' Across the field tramped the village philosopher, and before many weeks had passed a committee had been selected, the little theatre engaged, and the Sunday Evening Club of Northeast Harbor had begun its beneficent career, with its pleasant imitation of the greater assemblage. In Chicago a financial or political magnate reads from the Bible, a bishop or notable preacher offers

Frederic Illsley Phillips

prayer, and some important person, from far or near, addresses the crowd. At Northeast Harbor, on the other hand, a villager reads, a visiting minister prays, and the audience sings familiar hymns. Fortunately for the village, it is set in the most beautiful region of the New England coast, and as a natural consequence it happens in the course of a summer that almost every one of distinction in political or social movements, or in religious teaching, comes that way, and the supply of speakers is unfailing. Thus, for six seasons, and for ten weeks each year, the theatre has been thronged by city folk and villagers, old and young; workers in the shops, 'help' of the hotels; of various religious communions and of none; and the most competent of American citizens have been drafted to offer to this modest gathering the finest utterances of wisdom and piety. 'I have not missed one meeting in these six years,' said one of the leading men of the village, 'and it is the best thing that ever happened to Northeast Harbor.'

Captain Phillips was not only the first to visualize this ambitious scheme of communal service, but he soon revealed, in connection with it, a gift which he possessed in an almost unique degree. He was the best reader of the Bible I ever heard — not indeed as a textual critic or doctrinal expositor, but as a sheer lover of the Book which had been for forty years his daily guide and comforter. It was not a gift of intellectual interpretation but one of spiritual affinity. He read his chosen verses at the Sunday Evening Club as though they gave a sweet taste to his mouth, and parted with each admonition or counsel as though it were hard to leave it. In the Book of Revelation the Voice from Heaven speaks, saying: 'Go and take the little book which is open in the hand of the angel . . . and I took the little book out of the angel's hand, and ate it up; and it was in my mouth sweet as honey.' Such was Captain Phillips's feeling about the Bible. An angel had put it in his hand, and it was sweet as honey. In the purest sense of the word he was an old-fashioned Bible Christian. Yet this spiritual element did not rob him of humor. I said to him one Sunday evening: 'I wish you would come to Cambridge, Captain Phillips, and teach our young students for the ministry how to read the Bible,' and he answered me, with a friendly twinkle, 'Well, I should like the salary very much!'

The second communal enterprise to which Captain Phillips gave devoted service during the last years of his life has not yet reached its complete development; but in its character and ideal it provides a most instructive lesson for towns like Mt. Desert. There are four distinct villages in the township, ranging from a population of three hundred to thirty families. Each village has its own meeting-house for worship, and each has tried at various times to maintain its own minister. As a consequence, each has been able to pay a meagre wage, and could expect to obtain only the least effective of ministers; or if a competent man were secured, must anticipate soon surrendering him to a more stable pastorate. As a further consequence, each little church has had to struggle for its existence, and the influence of religion in village life has perceptibly declined. A distinguished American preacher of the last generation, on hearing that the churches of his city were but poorly attended, said, 'The people will come if you ring the bell loud enough'; but the diminishing congregations in the various villages of Mt. Desert during the hard days of winter had reached the point where one might have been led to say that the bells had stopped ringing altogether.

In 1925 there came to our notice the plan, already in operation elsewhere, known as 'The Larger Parish.' It proposed that two ministers, and perhaps a social worker in addition, should have the whole township as their charge, and by alternating in the conduct of worship, with the diligent use of one or two Ford cars, might oscillate between the various hamlets, taking the morning of Sunday in one and the afternoon in another; or again reversing the order; or yet again concentrating at one point in a union service. Here was, of course, a complete effacing of denominational lines and animosities. Indeed, the first pastor chosen for this work reported, after a winter of extraordinary efficiency, that no one had asked him what denomi-

nation he represented. Into this ambitious scheme,
Captain Phillips, still an unwavering Baptist, threw
himself with complete devotion, seeing in it, not only
a genuine expression of Christian unity, but the only
hope of restoring religion to its legitimate place in
communal life. His letters during the first winter
were jubilant in their statistical information. 'There
were eighty-nine out at Seal Harbor last Sunday,
though the weather was bad, and we determined to
beat that at Northeast Harbor in the evening, and
we had ninety-two.'

Serious problems, no doubt, still confront a scheme
which involves much coöperation and generosity. It
must contend with the sectarian jealousy which pre-
vails in small communities even more than in cities,
and with the sceptics who call themselves conservatives, and who resolutely maintain that no good thing
can come out of any unfamiliar Nazareth. Yet it
has become obvious that in many rural districts of
New England the choice must be made between a
practical paganism, promoted by ineffective and
divisive churches, and a Christianity which subordinates creed to character and sects to service.
As Benjamin Franklin said of the Colonies before the
Revolution, these little and deserted churches must
hang together or they will hang separately. The
summons of the time is from denominational contention to communal consecration, and many a seaside
village, now in grave danger from the invasion of city

Frederic Illsley Phillips

folk, and the contagion of moral laxity which is likely
to follow, may be saved from corruption by a Sunday
Evening Club and a Larger Parish.

Such is the contribution to social morality which
may be made by one plain and unassuming man in a
small town and in a small way. Most of the saints of
whom I have written were persons of importance
in the world, who have done great things in great
ways, and have overcome the temptations which
beset such lives, of pride, power, and self-display.
It may, however, be quite as difficult a task to redeem
village life from its besetting sins of indolence, light-
mindedness, and quarrelling, and to give it large
things to think of and a large work to do. After all,
it is from the life of the villages that the vitality of
the cities must be renewed, and a saint in Asticou may
become a savior of Chicago or New York. In President Eliot's study of John Gilley, the Mt. Desert
fisherman — a small pamphlet which Mr. Eliot once
said was the only writing of his which might hope to
have a permanent place as literature — he concludes
with these words: 'This is the life of one of the forgotten millions. It contains no material for distinction, fame, or long remembrance; but it does contain
the material and present the scene for a normal
human development, through mingled joy and sorrow, labor and rest, adversity and success, and
through the tender loves of childhood, maturity,
and age. We cannot but believe that it is just for

countless, quiet, simple lives like this that God made and upholds this earth.' The words might have been written of Frederic Phillips. Without such undistinguished, unambitious, and simple lives, promoting the welfare and inspiring the courage of the forgotten millions, God's purposes for this earth are not likely to be fulfilled.

CHAPTER XIV

CHARLES WILLIAM ELIOT

I HAVE recalled in these cursory sketches some of the men and women whom I have met at successive points of a long life, in its childhood, its youth, its education, its pastoral ministry, its academic service, and its advancing age. It is, as I said in the preface to these chapters, as if one of these guides stood, like a traffic officer, at each turning-point of decision or crossing of roads, to encourage or deter; so that in writing of them I have been led to retrace much of my own path of life. I cannot conclude this record without naming one other personal influence, which has directed or restrained many of the lives thus far considered, as well as my own, and without allusion to which these reminiscences would be without background or perspective.

It may seem quite inappropriate to include President Eliot's name among those of present-day saints. He would himself vehemently protest against such a title. Only a few months before his death I happened to remark to him that I was yielding to the propensity to reminiscence characteristic of old age, and was proposing to describe some of my acquaintances and friends under the title of present-day saints. 'Oh, not saints!' was Mr. Eliot's vigorous rejoinder. The implication of superior virtue, of self-conscious holiness, made the word 'saint' peculiarly obnoxious to his virile and outward-looking habit of mind. The saints, he felt, would never become saintly until they forgot their saintliness. I had no opportunity during the last weeks of his failing vitality to demonstrate to him the unhistorical nature of his view of sainthood, or to assure him that the moralist Saint James had as legitimate a place in the New Testament as the mystic Saint John, or that Jerome editing the Vulgate, and Christopher helping travellers across a stream, had been as justifiably canonized as Antony fleeing to the desert or Catherine of Siena in her contemplative ecstasies.

When therefore I review the lives which have pointed out the direction or smoothed the hard places of the Christian way, I must permit myself a few words of reference to the one I have known longest and best. The story of its official career will be in due time adequately told, and I have no intention of anticipating that record of educational and civic leadership. Within this sphere of conspicuous service, however, there was an inner life of spiritual dedication and conviction, which was disguised by austerity of manner, but was in reality the source of his fearless decisions and his firmness of will. It is this fundamentally religious nature, in a man much involved in temporal affairs, to which I may now briefly testify, though such disclosure of his spiritual experience would have seemed to him in his life-

Charles W. Eliot

time an invasion of a carefully guarded stronghold of reticence.

I was only ten years old when Charles Eliot became, not only an elder brother, but in many ways a paternal guide; and this intimacy, diminished during his public career, was happily renewed in his last years, and was never so close and confidential as at the end. Thus for a period of nearly seventy years I have had the opportunity of observing some aspects of his life which were not conspicuously revealed, and whose very existence was by many critics unsuspected.

The popular impression of President Eliot was, I suppose, that of a singularly cold and even severe personality, in which the gentler traits of character were quite subordinate, or even non-existent. He had inherited the traditions of the Puritans, and had been trained in the habits of a man of science. Partly through inherited temperament, and partly because of a congenital blemish which marked his face, he had acquired, even in youth, a rigidity of manner which might easily be mistaken for lack of emotion or sympathy. To some observers of his public life he seemed to be little more than an engine of energy, a steam-roller of educational progress, crushing opposition and levelling the way; and it is quite true that his official duties confirmed in him the inclination to express himself by acts rather than by words. Being told for instance, one day, after the death of his elder son, of the sympathy offered by the staff of the Library, he expressed his regret that the happiness of intimacy with these assistants had been denied him, because it was so difficult to detach personal kindliness from official assurance. Having the destinies of so many colleagues at his command, he must, he thought, in large part, leave unexpressed his affection or esteem.

This habitual attitude of restraint may be illustrated by his extraordinary moderation in the use of language. In a lifelong intimacy, covering every kind of experience, in sorrow and joy, exasperation and misinterpretation, I never but once heard President Eliot use a profane word; and that instance remains a vivid, as well as an amusing, reminiscence. When a boy of about fourteen years I was sailing with him in a small sloop along the Beverly shore. A violent squall struck us, we were abruptly dismasted, and the sails and rigging went over the side. In the midst of this confusion and peril my skipper astounded me by ejaculating, 'The devil!' and I remember this awful utterance as more bewildering and alarming than the fury of the gale.

Thus it happened that temperamental tendencies conspired with official responsibilities, and with the vicissitudes of domestic life, to detach Mr. Eliot from dependence on others in his judgments and conclusions. He was companionable in habit, but solitary in spirit. Even at the height of his public career,

Charles William Eliot

when he was surrounded by every testimony of confidence and honor, the number of his intimate friends was very limited, and his decisions were for the most part made without counsel or reënforcement. This isolation of experience, however, makes all the more impressive the evidences of moral obligation and spiritual vitality exhibited, not in professions of piety, but in ways of conduct and thought. He had been bred in the reverent atmosphere of his parents' church and home, and was throughout his life an habitual attendant at worship and a communicant at the Lord's Supper; training his children, as he had been trained, in a rational and undogmatic faith. He dissented, it is true, from most of the creeds of the dominant churches of Christendom, and of some of them he did not hesitate to speak with reprobation, or even with abhorrence. As a consequence, his non-conformity was frequently interpreted as heresy, and his faith as unbelief. His undiguised candor often gave offence, as when, with fine precision of language, he told an assemblage of preachers that their work seemed to him characterized by 'intellectual frugality.' I have even heard an intelligent woman quoted as saying that little religion could be expected at Harvard University while its president was an atheist. Within this appearance of detachment or severity, however, there was a controlling sense of vocation and guidance which made him immune to criticism or censure. Nothing could be more repulsive to him than any pose of piety or assumption of saintliness; but the calmness of his judgments and the clearness of his vision indicated a consciousness of spiritual authority, as though he repeated to himself the great words, 'My meat is to do the will of Him that sent me.'

At this point is disclosed also the secret of the extraordinary confidence with which President Eliot expressed his conclusions, — an assurance which seemed to some critics the evidence of vanity or arrogance. Nothing human seemed beyond his province. Political, economic, social, ethical, and religious problems, were interpreted, defended, or attacked by him as though he were their appointed advocate or prosecutor. This habit of mind, which had an appearance of self-assertion, was in fact promoted by self-forgetfulness. He was sure of himself because he did not care for himself. No consideration of advantage or reputation had the least weight with him, if only he could contribute to what he thought was right or check what he thought was wrong. The Germans describe such a character as *Selbstlos*, and President Eliot, with continuity and consistency, illustrated this quality of selflessness — a complete emancipation from self-seeking, and a not less complete indifference to opposing opinions when he believed he had a just cause to maintain. Moral timidity is as a rule a sign of self-consideration; one is thinking how the act or word may affect his own security or influence. President Eliot's courage was not self-display, but self-effacement; not the audacity of vanity, but the fearlessness of faith.

It might seem sufficient evidence of President Eliot's religious convictions to recall the two notable transitions which have already been described, and which were accomplished through his initiative. The detachment of theological teaching from sectarianism opened the way toward Christian unity; the emancipation of worship from compulsion gave a new meaning to religion in the University. These external changes might, however, be credited by a critical observer to Mr. Eliot's sagacity and diplomacy rather than to his personal religion. Theology must be made scientific or be dismissed from consideration in a university; worship must be made free, or abandoned as, in the words of the young petitioners for liberty, 'repugnant' and 'unjust.'

When, however, one turns from these administrative achievements to the candid utterances in which President Eliot habitually expressed his thought, it is difficult to question the reality of his moral idealism and reverent faith. In writing of Phillips Brooks I called attention to the fact that a preacher frequently reveals his inner life more undisguisedly in the pulpit than in ordinary conversation. A sense of anonymousness, as prophet or priest, may permit one to say in preaching or prayer what he might shrink from saying in his own person. One may feel — sometimes without much justification — that his message has been given him to speak. Something of this escape from self-consciousness is to be observed in many writings of President Eliot. When called on to make his profession of faith, or to give his counsel to the young, his candor quite overcomes his reticence, and he does not hesitate to report without disguise the secret of his serenity and strength.

Each study of character, or address of personal counsel, rises at its close to a statement, brief and restrained but direct and cogent, of the place of religion in a normal and happy human life. Thus, in describing the 'Religion of the Future' he says : 'It sees evidence in the moral history of the human race that a loving God rules the universe. Trust in this supreme rule is personal consolation and support under many human trials and sufferings. . . . The future religion will have the attribute of universality, and of adaptability to the rapidly increasing stores of knowledge and power over nature acquired by the human race. . . . It will have its saints, but its canonization will be based on grounds somewhat new. It will have its heroes ; but they must have shown a loving, disinterested, or protective courage. It will have its communions with the Great Spirit, with the spirits of the departed, and with living fellow-men of like minds. . . . Finally, this twentieth-century religion is not only to be in harmony with the great secular movements of modern society — democracy, individualism, social idealism, the zeal for education, the spirit of research, the modern tendency to welcome the new, the fresh powers of preventive medicine, and the recent advances in business and industrial ethics — but also in essential agreement with the direct, personal teachings of Jesus, as they are reported in the Gospels. The revelation he gave to mankind thus becomes more wonderful than ever.'

Or again, in writing of the 'Education of Boys and Girls' : 'Perfect freedom of thought is not only consistent with the sincerest piety, but it is really the only atmosphere in which the holiest piety can grow.' Or again, in 'The Crying Need of a Renewed Christianity' : 'True Christianity is not a body of doctrine, or an official organization to direct and control men's minds and wills. It is a way of life.' Or yet once more, in defining 'Progressive Liberalism in the Closing and the Opening Century,' he says, 'Let no man fear that reverence and love for Jesus will diminish as time goes on. . . . Already we see signs of the approaching fulfilment of Whittier's prophecy :

'"Our Friend, our Brother, and our Lord,
    What may thy service be?
    Nor name nor form nor ritual word,
    But simply following thee."'

With the same undisguised candor, in his address in 1917 at Symphony Hall, on 'A Free and Open Christian Church,' he announces in glowing language the articles of his creed :

'We believe in a loving God who inspires and vivifies the universe, and to that God we attribute in an infinite degree all the finest, noblest, sweetest, loveliest qualities which human nature embodies and displays in finite forms. For us God is not a despotic ruler, a judge, just or unjust, or a lord of embattled hosts. He is for us a Father Divine; and the word "father" signifies for us the best human combination of justice, tenderness, and intimate sympathy. . . .

'With all our hearts we believe in, and would fain imitate the Good Samaritan, the father of the prodigal son, Martha and Mary, especially Martha' — (a characteristic touch) — 'the publican who would not so much as lift up his eyes unto heaven, the poor widow who cast in two mites, and that disciple whom Jesus loved, and to whom he said as he hung on the cross, "Behold thy mother!" And from that hour the disciple took her to his own home.

'We believe most earnestly and completely in the Beatitudes, the Lord's Prayer, and the rule, "Whatsoever ye would that men should do to you, do ye even so to them."

'We believe that all men need to reverence, to worship, and to love.

'We believe in the spiritual interpretations and sanctions of duty, obligation, and responsibility.

'We believe that to whom much is given, of them much is expected or required; and that the sense of obligation is strongest in a grateful conscience.

Charles William Eliot

'Therefore, we mean and try to love God and our neighbor, to love mercy, to help the desolate and the wronged, to seek the truth, and, finding any, to speak it and act it out.'

These formal and public statements would seem to indicate sufficiently the nature and scope of President Eliot's religious faith. A more convincing evidence was provided by his habitual and inconspicuous conduct of daily life in his home and in the world. Being left a widower when but thirty-five years old, he applied himself to the religious education of his little boys, not, by the way of catechisms and creeds, but by that of literature and life. Each Sunday evening they recited the great lyrics of religious faith, committed to heart as well as to memory. Each morning, on the sloop where the family spent the summer during the first years of his administration, the drowsy crew was waked by his resonant bass voice summoning them to join in the morning hymn:

> 'Again the Lord of life and light
> Awakes the kindling ray,
> Unseals the eyelids of the morn
> And pours increasing day.'

This way of approach to religion through its lyric expression was later defended by him as appropriate for childhood. 'It takes an adult,' he wrote, 'with a tendency to metaphysics to get anything out of a catechism. Will not a child unconsciously get religion out of poetry, if it be well-selected? . . . Bryant's "Water-Fowl,"' he goes on, 'is the simplest possible presentation to a child's mind of the loving fatherhood of God. . . . I believe it [such instruction] can be given with pleasure to the child, and with delight to the parent. I am sure of the latter, for I have tried it.'

An even more convincing, though less conspicuous, evidence of President Eliot's substantial faith was provided, to those who stood near him, by his intimate concern for the problems and sorrows of his colleagues and friends. He was not given to profuse utterances of sympathy, or gifted in the finer arts of emotional consolation; but when it came to a real emergency, and a steadying hand was sought, then, with a precision and effectiveness never forgotten by those whom it reached, the healing word was spoken, or the wisely directed aid was applied; and there seemed fulfilled the prophecy of the Hebrew seer that a man should be as a hiding-place from the tempest and as the shadow of a great rock in a weary land. The son of a professor suddenly dies, and the words of the president have the strengthening touch of one who has found his own way through the same darkness to the light. A family within the college circle is abruptly thrown into destitution, and relief comes from the friend who had seemed remote and austere. A contagious disease invades a home, and the whole household is transported to the president's house. It was an individualized service which thus applied itself, not so much to the offering of sympathy as to the revival of courage. Every man, the Apostle wrote, must bear his own burden; but the strength to bear one's own burden is best attained, as the same teacher says, by bearing the burden of others. That was the Christian paradox which President Eliot expressed in his classic letter to President Wilson, when by a tragic coincidence Mrs. Wilson died at the very moment when the Nation was on the brink of war. 'Under such circumstances,' wrote President Eliot, 'there is comfort and relief for the sufferer in resolving that he will thereafter do everything in his power to help other people who are suffering or bereaved. . . . In such an effort you would find great consolation.'

It is not necessary to dwell further on this aspect of President Eliot's character, which may have been disguised to some observers by his administrative energy and civic courage. The veil was rarely lifted; but when occasions of sorrow or disaster occurred there was disclosed the sustaining strength of a rational and fortifying faith. Thus, after the sudden and tragic death of his son, when President Eliot was driving to the funeral at King's Chapel, he turned to his companion and said: 'We must now try to think of the many people who are happy to-day'; and when, two years later, a young relative suddenly died, President Eliot wrote to the stricken father, 'We must now so live as to be worthy of the young lives that are gone.'

The voluminous biography of his son is not only the record of a young man of rare gifts and professional distinction, but an undesigned revelation of the father's character; and at the close of this appealing volume the son's religious faith is thus described: 'He was by temperament reflective . . . and had an inquiring mind, which sought causes and uniform sequences. He was therefore naturally religious, but not in any emotional, conventional, or ecclesiastical sense. His creed was short and simple. He believed that a loving God rules the universe, and that the path to loving and serving Him lies through loving and serving men; and that the way to worship Him is to revere the earthly beauty, truth, and goodness He has brought forth.' The words thus applied to another have in them an unconscious touch of spiritual autobiography, and reveal within President Eliot's reticence and austerity the same short and simple creed. He believed, as he wrote of his dear son, that a loving God rules the universe, and that the path to loving and serving Him lies through loving and serving men. The eulogy of the son so early lost might well serve as the father's epitaph.